WALKER'S COMPANION

NORTH YORK MOORS

WALKER'S COMPANION

NORTH YORK MOORS

MALCOLM BOYES and
HAZEL CHESTER

Photography by David Ward

TED SMART

ACKNOWLEDGMENTS

We would like to thank the following people for their assistance during the preparation of *Walker's Companion: North York Moors*:

Frank Duerden for initial confidence in us and continued support throughout.

Alan and Olive Chester for their help with transport and for providing refreshments on a number of walks.

Betty Hood for her assistance with literature and ideas.

Alan Staniforth for general information on the National Park.

Anne Harrison for her help in updating this book.

John Goodman, Footpaths Officer for the National Park, and the National Park Rangers for checking the routes for problems or diversions.

Miss C. R. Tracey, District Forester with the Forestry Commission, for help and information.

Mark Feather for his patience, help and assistance with details about the wildlife on the North York Moors.

Bob Dicker, Warden for the National Trust, for checking the route of the Bridestones walk.

The Countryside Commission for permission to use material from their publications (The Countryside Access Charter).

Ordnance Survey for permission to use their Outdoor Leisure maps.

Finally, we would like to extend our special thanks and congratulations to David Ward, whose splendid photographs have captured the spirit of the North York Moors.

This edition produced for
The Book People Ltd,
Hall Wood Avenue,
Haydock,
St Helens WA11 9UL

First published in 1995 by Ward Lock

Printed and bound in Spain by Graficromo S.A.,Cordoba

ISBN 0-7063-7350-2

Contents

Introduction 6

The North York Moors National Park 8

Facts and Figures 9

Selected Walks in the North York Moors National Park

Introduction to the route descriptions 12

Selected routes in order of increasing difficulty:

1. EASY ROUTES
1. The White Horse Walk 16

2. The Bridestones 19

3. Farndale's Daffodil Walk 22

4. The Rosedale Iron Mine Trail 26

5. Beggar's Bridge and the Esk Valley 30

6. A Smuggler's Way 34

7. Ancient and Modern Trackways 39

8. The Hole of Horcum 45

2. MODERATE ROUTES
9. Osmotherley and the Drove Road 50

10. Hackness and Whisperdales 54

11. A Shipwreck Trail 58

12. The Packhorse Tracks of Commondale Moor 64

13. The Levisham Circuit 69

14. The Cleveland Hills 73

15. The Captain Cook Circuit 77

16. The Scenery of Robin Hood's Bay 83

17. Danby Moors 88

3. MORE STRENUOUS ROUTES
18. The Bilsdale Head Circuit 94

19. The Heritage Coast Path 100

20. The Farndale Head Circuit 106

21. Helmsley Circuit 114

Appendices
Access for the walker 124

Safety 124

Giving a grid reference 125

Countryside Access Charter 126

Addresses of useful organizations 127

Index 128

INTRODUCTION

In selecting the walks for this book we have chosen those with good views and a variety of scenery—moorland, forestry, fields, woods and coastline. We then looked for places and items of interest to enhance the walks. As you walk these routes you may be treading in the steps of smugglers, or a carrier with his packhorse ponies, visiting the iron mines of a century ago or see the sites of shipwrecks and dramatic rescues off this rugged coastline.

The selection of routes which we have included in this book has given us a great deal of pleasurable walking. The longest walks were done in sections simply because we couldn't complete them in a day and take the detailed notes and information required. Initially our early walks were undertaken with snow on the ground. We met and talked with farmers digging sheep out of snow-drifts who then carried them away to let them recuperate from their ordeal in the farm buildings. In contrast, the Bilsdale Head Circuit with its exposed route was completed on one of the windiest days of the year. There were extremely fine views across the top of Hasty Bank but, as we remarked to a walker going the other way, 'Someone must have left a door open, there's a heck of a draught'! We returned back over the Cleveland Hills on one of the hottest days of the summer—the only thing that spurred us on was the thought of an ice-cream at the finish.

We enjoyed the colour of the wild flowers in Hilda Wood near Hackness and around Hayburn Wyke on the coast. Yellowhammers flitted through the bushes near Levisham, buzzards wheeled over Sleights Moor, grey and white wagtails bobbed around the stream in Hackness and tufted duck swam on Staindale Lake. As you set out on any of these walks it is worthwhile slipping a pair of binoculars into your rucksack, together with guidebooks on birds and wild flowers — it can increase your pleasure tremendously.

Most people will be walking these routes in summer and early autumn, possibly when the purple heather is in bloom; however, other times of the year can be equally rewarding. In early spring the trees burst into leaf and a carpet of bluebells and primroses offer a variety of colour. The daffodils alongside the River Dove in Farndale are known nationally. In winter, on a fine crisp day, the views can be spectacular. All these walks can be undertaken at virtually any time of the year, provided you are adequately clothed and equipped.

If you are inexperienced, start off with the easy walks in this book in summer. Then work through to the longer, more strenuous walks, and go back to the easier walks for a winter outing. Follow the advice in the chapter on safety and go well-equipped. If an emergency does arise you should then be aware of what to do. We hope you get as much pleasure out of these walks as we have.

Ravenscar from Stoupe Beck

THE NORTH YORK MOORS NATIONAL PARK

John Dower defined a National Park as 'an extensive area of beautiful and relatively wild country in which, for the nation's benefit and by appropriate national decision and action, (a) the characteristic landscape beauty is strictly preserved, (b) access and facilities for public open-air enjoyment are amply provided, (c) wild life and buildings and places of architectural and historic interest are suitably protected, while (d) established farming use is effectively maintained.'

The United Kingdom lagged behind many other countries of the world in the establishment of its National Parks; Argentina, Canada (which has the largest national park extending to over 11 million acres), Germany, Italy, New Zealand, Poland, South Africa, Spain, Sweden, Switzerland and the United States were among the countries which had National Parks before any were designated here.

Under the National Parks and Access to the Countryside Act of 1949 a National Parks Commission was established, which was responsible for the creation of National Parks; ten were created by the Commission in England and Wales between 1950 and 1957. In 1968 the National Parks Commission was replaced by the Countryside Commission, which therefore took over responsibility for the Parks. A further change came under the Local Government Act of 1972; under this Act a separate National Park Authority was set up in each National Park, charged with its administration. Each Authority was given the task of producing a National Park Plan by 1 April 1977 and of reviewing that plan at intervals of not more than five years. This set out the policies of the Authority for the management of its Park and proposals for carrying out these policies.

The National Park Authorities are charged with two main aims. The first is to preserve and enhance the natural beauty of the areas designated as National Parks, the second is to encourage the provision or improvement of facilities for the enjoyment of open-air recreation and the study of nature within the Parks. They must in addition have due regard for the social and economic needs of the people living within the Parks.

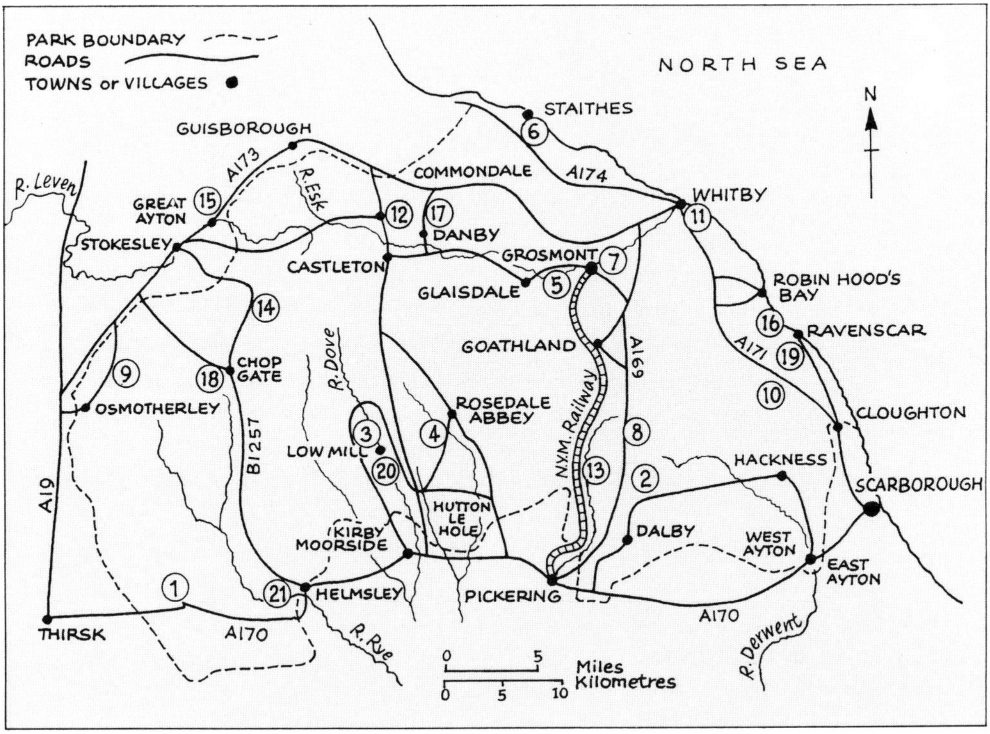

FIGURE 1 *The North York Moors National Park, showing the Park boundary, major roads, towns and villages and the location of routes*

The overall management of the North York Moors National Park is the responsibility of North Yorkshire County Council, as approximately 96% of the Park lies within the county, the remainder being situated in County Cleveland. The Park is governed by a committee of twenty-seven members, eighteen of whom are County or District Councillors, and nine members appointed by the Secretary of State for the Environment. A staff of full and part-time workers under the overall control of the National Park Officer are responsible for implementing the decisions of the Park Committee. The National Park Authority receives 75% of its revenue from Central Government (Department of Environment Supplementary Block Grant Countryside Commission) and 25% from local rates.

Some Facts and Figures about the North York Moors National Park

DESIGNATED

28 November 1952. This was the sixth National Park to be designated.

AREA

553 square miles (143226 hectares). This is the fourth largest National Park after the Lake District, Snowdonia and the Yorkshire Dales.

LAND OWNERSHIP (%)
Private land 76.5
Forestry Commission 16.5
Water Authorities 4
National Park Authority 2
National Trust 1

POPULATION
On the basis of recent census data the resident population of the Park is estimated at 25,253. The trend over the last fifty years is for villages in the centre of the Park to decline while those on the edge, which can be used as commuter bases, have increased.

TOURISTS
A roadside survey in 1980 indicated that on a fine summer Sunday there would be 137,000 visitors to the Park. An estimated 11.14 million recreational visits are made to the Park each year.

WHERE THE VISITORS COME FROM (% 1986)
England
North Yorkshire 16.9
Cleveland 18.5
West and South Yorkshire and Humberside 19.2
Durham, Tyne and Wear 5.6
Cumbria and Lancashire 3.8
Eastern and Southern England 24.2
Scotland 1.4
Wales, West Midlands and West of England 7.5
Overseas 2.9

SELECTED WALKS IN THE
NORTH YORK MOORS
NATIONAL PARK

Roseberry Topping

INTRODUCTION TO THE
ROUTE DESCRIPTIONS

1. ACCESS (see page 124)
The routes described later have been walked for a long time without objection and it is not expected that any difficulties will be encountered. Nevertheless, they do in some cases cross country over which there is, strictly speaking, no legal right of way, and in such cases the responsibility must lie with the walker to obtain any necessary permission before crossing such land. In particular, 'short cuts' should not be taken that could cause annoyance to local people. If you encounter an obstruction or difficulty you should contact the National Park Office at Helmsley (see Addresses) for paths within the National Park.

2. ASCENT
The amount of climbing involved in each route has been estimated from Outdoor Leisure maps and should be regarded as approximate only.

3. CAR-PARKS
The walks start from a car-park or a village or town where parking will be possible. Do not block farm gateways or narrow roads with indiscriminate parking.

4. INTERESTING FEATURES
The best position for seeing these is indicated both in the route descriptions and on the maps by (1), (2), etc. A wide variety of subjects is included.

5. LENGTH
These are strictly 'map miles' estimated from the Outdoor Leisure maps; no attempt has been made to take into account any ascent or descent involved.

6. MAPS
The maps are drawn to a scale of approximately 1:25 000 (see Figure 1) and all names are as given on the Outdoor Leisure maps. Field boundaries should be taken as a 'best description'. The maps have been drawn in the main, so that the route goes from the bottom to the top of the page. This will enable the reader to 'line up' the map whilst still holding the book in the normal reading position. The arrow on each map points to grid north. The scale of some small features has been slightly

12

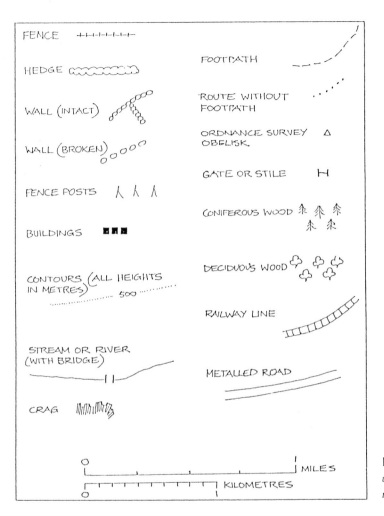

FENCE

HEDGE

WALL (INTACT)

WALL (BROKEN)

FENCE POSTS

BUILDINGS

CONTOURS (ALL HEIGHTS IN METRES) 500

STREAM OR RIVER (WITH BRIDGE)

CRAG

FOOTPATH

ROUTE WITHOUT FOOTPATH

ORDNANCE SURVEY OBELISK

GATE OR STILE

CONIFEROUS WOOD

DECIDUOUS WOOD

RAILWAY LINE

METALLED ROAD

MILES

KILOMETRES

FIGURE 2 *Symbols used on detailed route maps*

exaggerated for clarity. For easy cross-reference, the relevant Outdoor Leisure and Landranger sheets are indicated on each map.

The letters 'L' and 'R' stand for left and right respectively. Where these are used for changes of direction then they imply a turn of about 90° when facing in the direction of the walk. 'Half L' and 'half R' indicate a half-turn, i.e. approximately 45°, and 'back half L' or 'back half R' indicate three quarter-turns, i.e. about 135°. PFS stands for 'Public Footpath Sign', PBS for 'Public Bridleway Sign' and OS for 'Ordnance Survey'.

To avoid constant repetition, it should be assumed that all stiles and gates mentioned in the route description are to be crossed (unless there is a specific statement otherwise).

7. ROUTE DESCRIPTION

Nothing remains constant—the information given, as far as is known, was accurate when collected, but inevitably hedges can be removed, and new wire fences and gates set up. Official diversions of paths are always well waymarked.

8. STANDARD OF THE ROUTES

The briefest examination of the route descriptions that follow will show that the routes described cover an enormous range of both length and of difficulty; some of the easy routes at least can be undertaken by a family party, with care, at almost any time of the year, while the hardest routes are more suitable for experienced fell-walkers who are both fit and well-equipped. Any walker therefore who is contemplating following a route should make sure before starting that it is within their ability.

It is difficult in practice, however, to assess the difficulty of any route, because it depends on a number of factors and will in any case vary considerably from day to day with the weather. Any consideration of weather conditions must, of course, be left to the walker (but read the section on safety first). Apart from that, it is probably best to attempt an overall assessment of difficulty based upon the length, amount of ascent and descent, problems of route-finding and finally, upon the roughness of the terrain.

Each of the routes has therefore been given a grading based upon a consideration of these factors. A general description of each grade follows:

Easy (1) Generally short walks (up to 5 miles, 8 km) over well-defined paths, with no problems of route-finding. Some climbing may be involved, but progress is over fairly gradual slopes with only short sections of more difficult ground. The paths may, however, sometimes run along cliffs, streams or steep slopes, where care should be taken.

Moderate (2) Rather longer walks (up to about 10 miles, 16 km)

Urra Moor from Hasty Bank

mostly over paths, but with sections where route-finding may be more difficult.

More strenuous (3) Perhaps longer walks 10–20 miles, 16–32 km) some with prolonged spells of climbing.

The walks are arranged in order of increasing difficulty so that Route 1 is the easiest and Route 21 the hardest. Finally, a summary of each walk is given at the head of each section with information on the distance, amount of climbing and any special difficulties, such as, for example, the need to use a compass on featureless moorland that will be met on the way.

9. STARTING AND FINISHING POINTS

The majority of walks are circular in order to avoid any problems with transport when the walk is completed. The location of each starting and finishing point is given by the number of the appropriate Landranger (1:50 000) map with a six-figure grid reference (see page 125; thus (100-515830) indicates grid reference 515830 which can be found on Landranger sheet no. 100. The starting points are also shown on Figure 1. The Landranger and Outdoor Leisure sheets required for each route are given on the appropriate route maps—ensure that you are carrying all the sheets required, as a route may go over more than one.

The usual method of estimating the length of time needed for a walk is by Naismith's Rule; 'For ordinary walking allow one hour for every three miles (5 km) and add one hour for every 2000 feet (600 m) of ascent; for backpacking with a heavy load allow one hour for every 2½ miles (4 km) and one hour for every 1500 feet (450 m) of ascent'. However, for many this tends to be over-optimistic and it is better for each walker to form an assessment of his own performance over one or two walks. Naismith's Rule also makes no allowance for rest or food stops or for the influence of weather conditions.

10. TIME FOR COMPLETION

A number of the starting points for the walks can be reached by using the two scenic railway lines which cross the moors. Routes 7 and 13 can be walked in conjunction with the diesel and steam-hauled North York Moors Railway between Pickering and Grosmont. The Esk Valley Railway operated by British Rail from Middlesbrough to Whitby can be used for Routes 5, 7, 11, 12, 15 and 17.

11. RAILWAYS

1.1

THE WHITE HORSE WALK

STARTING AND FINISHING POINT
Sutton Bank car-park (100-515830) on the A170 from Helmsley to Thirsk.

LENGTH
3¼ miles (5 km)

ASCENT
200 feet (60 m)

This short walk offers some of the finest views in Yorkshire. From 900 feet (270 m) up on the edge of the moors you can see across the Vale of York to the mountains of the Yorkshire Dales. The route is obvious throughout the walk and the climb and descent are along stepped paths.

ROUTE DESCRIPTION (Map 1)

From the car-park near the Information Centre, cross over the main road and turn R towards the edge of the escarpment. Turn L along the track beside the wire fence. A path leads off here to the view indicator (*1*) if you wish to visit this point. Continue on the track beside the wire fence and you soon find yourself walking along the top of a cliff.

Below and to the R is Lake Gormire (*2*), nestling among the trees, and beneath you is the steep hill descending to Thirsk (*3*). Continue along the cliff top for about ¾ mile (1.2 km), then fork R down the steps. At the bottom bear L on the path which offers views of the crags and continue on the main track which gradually sweeps L through mixed woodland to a gate into a car-park.

Above you at this point is the vast Kilburn White Horse (*4*). At the foot of a series of steps are two memorials to the building and maintenance of the White Horse. Climb the steps and turn L at the top passing above the White Horse. From this point there is an excellent view south (*5*). Follow the cliff-top path back to Sutton Bank car-park. On your R is the glider station with sailplanes often soaring overhead.

1 View indicator

From this excellent view-point the indicator points out the directions of numerous places, including Knaresborough Castle nineteen miles (30 km) away, Richmond twenty-four miles (39 km) and Great Whernside on the skyline thirty-two miles (52 km) to the west.

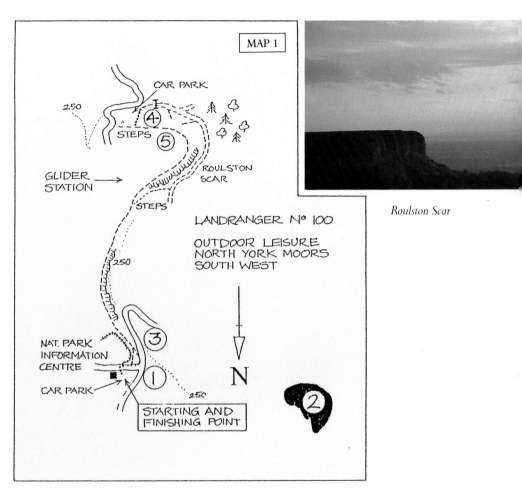

Roulston Scar

2 *Lake Gormire*
   The lake is set below the steep crags of Whitestone Cliff. It is
   an unusual lake, as it has no feeder stream or outlet and
   according to local folk lore is bottomless. The Garbutt Wood
   Nature Trail from Sutton Bank car-park explores the area
   above the lake.

3 *Sutton Bank Hill*
   Nowadays the steep 1 in 4 hill is used regularly by vehicles
   heading to and from the moors and coast, but in the 1920s
   the hill was used for motor trials with only the best men and
   machines reaching the top.

4 *Kilburn White Horse*
   The massive hill figure is 314 feet (95 m) long and 229 feet
   (70 m) high and was cut out on the hillside in 1857. It was
   the idea of Thomas Taylor and John Hodgson, the village

Kilburn White Horse

schoolmaster, who with thirty-three local men marked out and cut the figure. Unlike the hill figures in southern England, the base is limestone, not chalk, so to keep its white colour it requires regular maintenance. The figure is visible up to seventy miles (113 km) away.

5 *The view-point*

Among the many things to be seen from this view-point is the picturesque village of Kilburn. It contains workshops and a museum dedicated to Robert Thompson, the master woodcarver, whose furniture carries a mouse as its trademark. Looking further afield, the view extends over the patchwork quilt of fields which was originally the Forest of Galtres, to York in the distance.

1.2

The Bridestones

The High and Low Bridestones are two series of rock outcrops which stand on open heather moorland owned by the National Trust. They have been carved by the wind and rain into unusual shapes. One of the stones, weighing many tons, stands on a narrow base. The approach to the stones is past Staindale Water and along the National Trust nature trail. The walk passes through mixed woodland offering an interesting variety of scenery in a very short distance.

Route Description (Map 2)

From the car-park follow the stream towards the lake *(1)* and turn R around the shore. The path climbs slightly to join a gravel

STARTING AND FINISHING POINT
Staindale car-park (94/101-883904). Take the Whitby road north from Thornton Dale, turning R after 1½ miles (2.5km) onto Dalby Forest Drive (toll road). After 5½ miles (9 km) car-park on R at sharp bend.

LENGTH
3 miles (5 km)

ASCENT
325 feet (100 m)

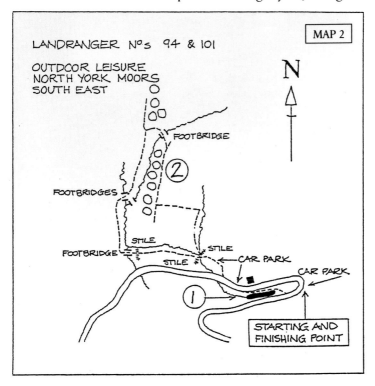

LANDRANGER Nºs 94 & 101

OUTDOOR LEISURE
NORTH YORK MOORS
SOUTH EAST

MAP 2

N

FOOTBRIDGE

②

FOOTBRIDGES

FOOTBRIDGE

STILE

STILE

CAR PARK

STILE

CAR PARK

①

STARTING AND
FINISHING POINT

path beside the toll road. Pass the toilets, turn half R across the car-park and follow the path to a National Trust Omega sign and two stiles. Pass over the stile on your R and into the wood.

The path climbs steeply through mixed woodland with a stream on the R. At the top of the hill there is a convenient seat offering a lovely view of the woodland. Follow the path which reaches open moorland and turn L at a yellow waymark arrow. Follow the track across the bracken and heather-covered moor to the Low Bridestones which appear on the skyline. Turn R at the first of the stones and follow the path passing about eight rock outcrops *(2)*.

Your path then descends into Bridestones Griff, a small stream fringed by trees, and sweeps back up the hillside to the High Bridestones. Take the path to the R to see all the Bridestones then return to the junction. Carry straight on along the ridge (i.e. to the L at the junction from your original direction) which offers views on your L, across the valley, to the Low Bridestones. The path eventually descends to a stream. Cross the footbridge on your R and follow the moorland valley keeping the stream on your L. A footbridge crosses the stream and leads to a stile into a field. The path swings L, following the edge of the wood to a stile. Bear half R down to the car-park you crossed earlier and retrace your steps around the lake back to the car-park.

1 *Staindale Water*
   This lake was created only a few years ago to attract a greater variety of wildlife to the area. You may see Canada geese, tufted duck or mallard on the lake and crossbills and siskin in the surrounding woodlands.

2 *The Bridestones*
   The Low Bridestones are the first group of rock outcrops encountered on the walk, the High Bridestones are to the north across Bridestones Griff. The fantastically shaped rocks have been sculptured by wind and water over some 60,000 years. The harder siliceous sandstone has resisted the erosion better than the less durable calcerous sandstone which has been washed away.

The Low Bridestones

1.3
FARNDALE'S DAFFODIL WALK

STARTING AND
FINISHING POINT
Low Mill car-park
(94/100-673952).
From Kirkbymoor-
side take the road
to Gillamoor and
continue on the
Hutton-le-Hole
road turning L to
Low Mill.

LENGTH
3½ miles (5.5 km)

ASCENT
200 feet (60 m)

This pleasant summer walk becomes a major tourist attraction in April when the wild daffodils bloom. A one-way system then operates on the narrow dales roads and extra fields are available for parking. Once on the walk and away from the traffic you will be able to enjoy the beauty of the daffodils and the rugged valley of Farndale.

ROUTE DESCRIPTION (Map 3)

From the car-park at Low Mill *(1)* take the path through the small gate (PFS to Church Houses) near the entrance. Walk down the paved way, cross over the footbridge and turn L. Follow the distinct path beside the River Dove for the next mile (1.6 km) *(2)*. The path eventually passes between a group of buildings *(3)* and bears R through a gate and on to Church Houses. Turn R and R again at the next two road junctions, then continue up the hill passing the church on your L. *(4)*.

Turn R 600 yards (550 m) beyond the last junction through a gate, keeping the wall on your L, to a stile. The next section sounds complicated, but the route is well signposted. Turn L over the stile and follow the hedge to a gate then continue above the farm buildings and along an access road. Bear half R (PFS)

Farndale churchyard

22

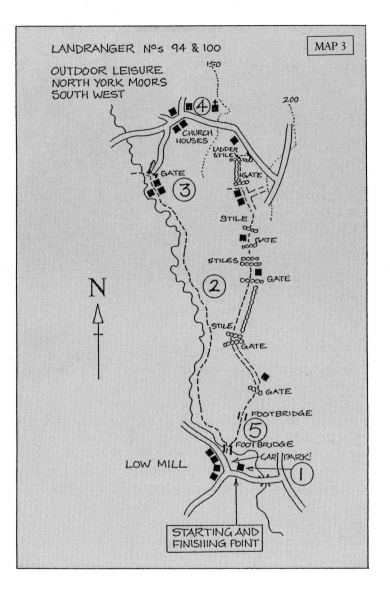

across the field to a stone stile and continue above Bitchagreen Farm. Pass through a gate and cross the field to a stile and then continue to a ladder stile. Bear half R over the field to a gate and continue on a paved way with a hedge on your L. Turn L at the stile and gate and cross the field into a farm lane. Turn R through a gate in the farmyard which leads to a stile and bridge over a stream; a paved way crosses the field (5) to the footbridge, which leads back to the car-park in Low Mill.

1 *Low Mill*

The hamlet takes its name from the water-powered mill erected in the middle of the nineteenth century. It ground corn until the 1930s and was used to generate electricity until 1956. The building has now been altered, but the leat along which the water was brought to power the mill can still be seen beside the River Dove.

2 *Wild Daffodils*

The banks of the River Dove offer a fine display of the wild daffodil (*Narcissus pseudonarcissus*), a native British plant. It has been dispersed along the river banks by various floods and can be found for about six miles (9.5 km). This is a nature reserve and it is an offence to pick or damage the plants.

3 *High Mill, Church Houses*

As you reach the buildings you pass two huge stone gateposts; one bears the inscription 'IG, IWF, JS, 1826'. The building on the R was a blacksmith's shop which was worked by James Kneeshaw in the 1890s. The next building was the corn mill powered by an overshot wheel receiving its water from Blakey Gill, a side stream of the River Dove. In the 1890s the miller was Mrs Ann Garbutt, but the mill ceased working about ten years later. The mill wheel and equipment were still in place about 1980.

4 *Farndale Church*

The church was built in 1831 on the site of an earlier church. It was restored between 1907 and 1914, when the west front was added. The churchyard contains a good display of daffodils in the season, probably transplanted over many years by local people.

5 *Paved ways* See page 32.

Banks of the River Dove

1.4

THE ROSEDALE IRON MINE TRAIL

STARTING AND
FINISHING POINT
Rosedale Abbey
Bank top (94/100-
721946). Turn
north off the A170
Helmsley to
Pickering road to
Hutton-le-Hole.
Turn R in the
village to
Lastingham then
fork L to Rosedale
Abbey Bank.

LENGTH
4¼ miles (7 km)

ASCENT
100 feet (30 m)

The picturesque valley of Rosedale was a busy centre of the iron mining trade which blossomed in the area from 1850. Nature has reclaimed the landscape but the remains of the buildings and the railway offer an interesting walk with excellent views. The route finding throughout the walk is simple.

ROUTE DESCRIPTION (Map 4)

From the small car-park at the top of the hill walk down the road *(1)*. Stop at the first bend where the road turns L; looking to the R you can see the bed of an inclined railway *(2)*, climbing to the road and continuing to your L to some ruined kilns.

Return back up the hill and turn R just before the car-park on a broad level track. On the L of the track you pass the ruins of an engine-house *(3)*. Continue on the track passing a group of cottages 50 yards (45 m) away on the R. The former railway track *(4)*, offers extensive views over Rosedale. After 2 miles (3 km) you reach the ruins of Sheriff's Pit *(5)*, set in a lonely position on the moor. From the railway track you can look NNE across the dale to the ruins of Rosedale East ironstone mines *(6)*. On no account cross the safety fence surrounding the shaft. Return back down the track to the car-park.

1 Rosedale Abbey Bank or Rosedale Chimney
   This 1 in 3 hill was used for hill climbs in the 1920s. The events were organized by the Bradford Motor Cycle and Light Car Club. The winner of the first event in 1921 was Arthur Champion who lived in Rosedale. Stones and tapes were set to force riders on to the steepest parts of the hill, which were then 1 in 2½. The hill was included in a number of motor trials but was eventually left out due to complaints.

2 Tramway and kilns
   To the R of the road you can see the tramway where ironstone was brought up from Hollins Mine. The tramway passed under the road and continued to the calcining kilns on

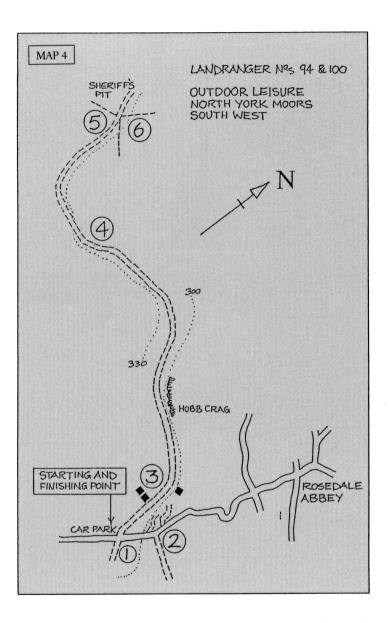

the L. A royalty of 6d (2½p) per ton was paid on the ironstone taken away, so to reduce the royalty and transport costs it was dropped into the kilns from above and roasted to drive off water and carbonic acid gas. Although not on a right of way, usually no objection is made to people visiting the kilns, but take care, as with any old buildings.

3 Engine-House and Rosedale Chimney

To raise the wagons some 400 feet (120 m) up the hillside on the tramway, three large low-pressure boilers were used to work the winding gear. The smoke from the boilers was taken away up a 50 feet (15 m) high chimney so as not to disturb the landowner's grouse. This was Rosedale Chimney; set high on the moors, it was a landmark for miles around but was demolished in 1972.

4 *Rosedale Mineral Railway*

The mineral railway was opened in 1861; it was a standard gauge single-track line from Battersby Junction, in the Leven Valley, to Bank Top, where you are, a distance of 14 miles (22.5 km). To reach the moor top from the north the wagons were drawn up a 1430 yard (1300 m) incline (see page 99). The line then came south skirting the edge of Farndale (see page 106) to Blakey Junction. The line then split, one spur coming south to Bank Top while the other contoured the head of Rosedale to the East Mines. For the railwaymen employed on the line it would be a hard life through the long winter. The line closed in 1929.

5 *Sheriff's Pit*

This pit operated like a coal mine. The men and horses entered the mine along an adit in the hillside. The ore was brought up the 270 feet (82 m) shaft to the surface and loaded straight onto wagons for transport to the ironworks. You can see the top of the shaft now surrounded by a fence for safety. This mine ceased operations in 1911.

6 *Rosedale East Mines*

Looking across the valley you can see the ruins of the kilns at Rosedale East Mines above the railway track. The mines started about 1858 and continued working until the General Strike of 1926.

Rosedale from Hobb Crag

1.5

BEGGAR'S BRIDGE AND THE ESK VALLEY

STARTING AND
FINISHING POINT
Egton Bridge (94-
803052). From the
A171 Whitby to
Guisborough road
turn L to Egton and
Egton Bridge.

LENGTH
3½ miles (5.5km)

ASCENT
400 feet (120 m)

The village of Egton Bridge is attractively set on the River Esk surrounded by woodlands. 1½ miles (2 km) to the west is Beggar's Bridge, a packhorse bridge. The walk which links these two places begins on a quiet road beside the River Esk leading to a field path which climbs over a ridge with fine views into the Esk Valley. The return is made through East Arncliff Wood along an ancient paved way.

ROUTE DESCRIPTION (Map 5)

From Egton Bridge walk along the road towards Glaisdale. The road follows the side of the river for ½ mile (800 m) then turns R under a railway bridge. Climb up the hill past Broom House Farm and after another 50 yards (45 m) turn L over a stile (PFS). Carry straight on, keeping the fenced woodland on your L. As you approach the stream turn L down some steps to a footbridge. If you look half R from the footbridge you can see your next stile into the wood at the top of the field. Cross the bridge and climb up the hill to the stile; looking back, there is a fine view of the wooded Esk Valley.

The path continues up through the conifers to a stile. Follow the edge of the field keeping the hedge on your L. There is a view straight ahead to the village of Glaisdale *(1)*. Carry straight on over a stile passing a television transmitter on your L. Continue straight on between the farm buildings to the road. The right of way bears L along the hedge, passes through another hedge and turns R to the road, but the farmer prefers walkers to use the route between the buildings. Turn L down the road—this is the 1 in 3 gradient Limber Hill which descends to the River Esk. Turn L at the junction at the foot of the hill and continue on past the road bridge along the river bank. After 30 yards (25 m) turn R over Beggar's Bridge *(2)*.

Pass under the railway bridge and cross the white footbridge in front of you, beside the ford. Climb up the stepped path *(3)* and through the woods above the river. A paved way climbs

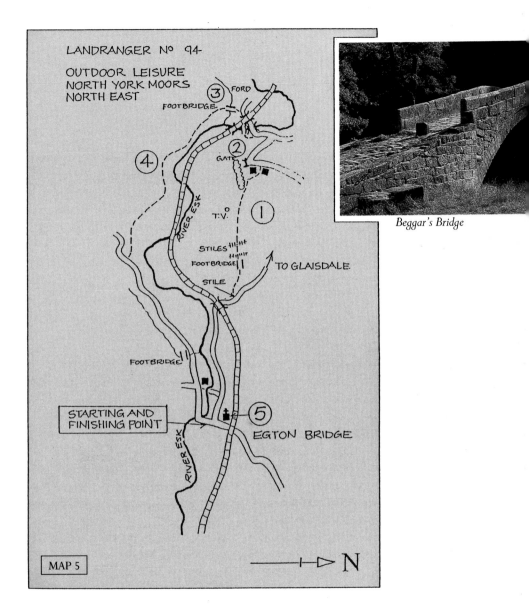

LANDRANGER Nº 94

OUTDOOR LEISURE
NORTH YORK MOORS
NORTH EAST

Beggar's Bridge

MAP 5

N

through the deciduous woodland *(4)* and eventually the track descends to a road. Turn L along the road and Egton Bridge Roman Catholic church comes into view *(5)*. The road follows Butter Beck for a while then bears R over a footbridge at the ford and continues along the road into Egton Bridge. Pass the Horseshoe Hotel and at the road junction turn L down a stepped path behind a white barrier. The path leads to a set of stepping stones across the river; walk up the lane and turn R down the road to your starting point. If the river is in flood, continue along the road and cross at the bridge.

1 *Glaisdale*

Across the fields you can see the terrace of houses rising up the hill beside the road. These were built for the ironstone workers who were employed when iron ore was discovered and mined from 1868. Three blast furnaces were built, but due to competition the mine closed in 1876.

2 *Beggar's Bridge*

The ancient packhorse bridge is now hemmed in between the railway and road bridges but is still attractively surrounded by woods. Thomas Ferris was a poor Egton lad who was courting Agnes Richardson, daughter of the squire. He was not acceptable, being from a poor family. Thomas decided to make his fortune at sea and acquired a position on a boat from Whitby. The night before he left he went to see Agnes but the river was in flood and as there was no bridge their tryst failed. Thomas did make a fortune, became Mayor of Hull and married Agnes. In 1619 he built Beggar's Bridge to prevent any other couple being parted by the river.

3 *'C to C and EVW' sign*

The sign indicates this path is on Alfred Wainwright's Coast to Coast Walk from St Bees Head in Cumbria to Robin Hood's Bay. The path is also used by walkers on the Esk Valley Way from the source of the River Esk to Whitby.

4 *Paved ways*

The paved ways were used by pannier ponies as the stones were wide enough for ponies but not for wheeled vehicles. The paved sections were usually on the steeper slopes, where traffic would erode the surface, but a few of them ran for miles across the moors. The ponies carried their loads in panniers balanced on either side of their backs. A train of twenty to forty ponies were usually headed by a lead pony wearing bells. Moorland coal was moved by this method around Rosedale as late as the 1870s.

5 *Egton Bridge Roman Catholic Church*

Egton Bridge was a centre of Catholicism when the religion was being suppressed in the seventeenth century. Father Nicholas Postgate was born in the village in 1599. In 1621 he was admitted to the seminary at Douai in France and became a priest. After serving various noted Catholic families in Yorkshire, he returned to the moors around Egton Bridge about 1660 and carried on his calling. In 1678 he was arrested for performing the duties of a priest, taken to York, tried and hanged at Tyburn.

Stepping stones at Egton Bridge

1.6

A SMUGGLER'S WAY

STARTING POINT
Straithes car-park
(94-781185) off the
A174 Whitby to
Saltburn road.

FINISHING POINT
Runswick lower
car-park
(94809159) off the
A174 Whitby to
Saltburn road.

LENGTH
3¾ miles (6 km)

ASCENT
425 feet (130 m)

Running south-eastwards from the picturesque village of Staithes for some three miles (5 km) are rugged cliffs rising to 330 feet (100 m). They give spectacular views out to sea and along the coastline itself, including the small harbour at Port Mulgrave, which is now being destroyed by the sea. Runswick is tucked away from view until the last minute, but the walk finally descends through the maze of paths in the village. The path is obvious throughout the walk.

ROUTE DESCRIPTION (Map 6)

From the car-park turn R down the road, which has restricted access for vehicles, and eventually descend into the cramped fishing village of Staithes (1). Follow the main road through the village to the Cod and Lobster Inn (2). Pass to the seaward side of the inn where there are views into the small harbour and across the Cowbar Nab. Just beyond the inn turn R up Church Street (3). The partly cobbled narrow road becomes a stepped path rising above the village. Turn L at the Cleveland Way sign, pass a farm on your R and continue on the distinct path across the fields (4), passing over four stiles.

There are fine marine views from the cliff top as the path climbs up towards Hinderwell Beacon (5). Continue along the cliff-top path until it enters Port Mulgrave and walk along the road. When the road turns R, inland, continue on the cliff-top path over a stile. To your L you can look down the cliff side to the small harbour of Port Mulgrave nestling at the foot of the cliffs (6). The outer arm of the harbour has been destroyed over the last twenty years by the action of the sea.

Eventually the path turns away from the small bay and continues along the spectacular coastline with the sea some 300 feet (90 m) below. Turn R at the sign to Runswick Bay, over a stile, and from there the path leads to a road junction. Turn L along Bank Top Lane, pass between the bollards and take the old road into Runswick (7). This gem of a village has been

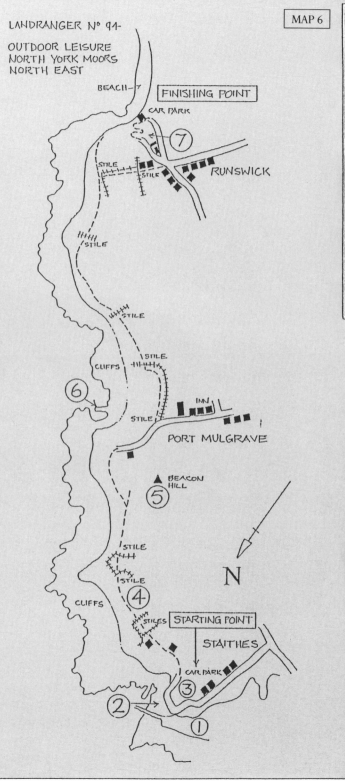

MAP 6

LANDRANGER Nº 94-

OUTDOOR LEISURE
NORTH YORK MOORS
NORTH EAST

BEACH

FINISHING POINT

CAR PARK

⑦

STILE

STILE

RUNSWICK

STILE

STILE

CLIFFS

STILE

⑥

INN

STILE

PORT MULGRAVE

▲ BEACON
HILL

⑤

STILE

STILE

④

CLIFFS

STILES

STARTING POINT

STAITHES

CAR PARK

③

②

①

N

First view of Runswick

Overleaf *Lingrow
Cliffs, Port Mulgrave*

35

hidden by the cliffs but now it begins to come into view. The old road, now a track, swings R and the rooftops appear. Fork L at some bollards onto a stepped path that soon turns R between the houses. The small gardens are usually a blaze of colour throughout the summer. The path descends towards the beach with side paths offering tempting opportunities to explore the village. The car-park is to the R of the village as you descend.

1 *Smuggling*

Smuggling was rife along the Yorkshire coast in the eighteenth and early nineteenth centuries and Staithes played a large part in the smuggling scene. It needs only a little imagination to think of a boatload of contraband being landed in Staithes Beck and taken along the narrow alleyways into the houses. The variety of smuggled goods brought into the country to avoid tax was amazing. As well as brandy and gin there were packs of playing cards, silk, spinning wheels, tea, chocolate, pepper and snuff. A network of people brought in the contraband, offloaded the boats, carried the goods inland and sold them to the public. To combat this trade there were armed revenue cutters patrolling the coast, but the smuggling ships were also heavily armed. The revenue men on the coast were sometimes assisted by the army; for example, in 1775 sixteen dragoons were stationed on the coast with a sergeant and an officer, four were at Staithes, two at Runswick and two more at Hinderwell. There were seven at Robin Hood's Bay with the sergeant and two at Sandsend, north of Whitby. The distribution of men gives an indication of the places where smuggling was most of a problem.

2 *The Cod and Lobster Inn*

The inn overlooks the sea, and this exposed position has caused the inn to be washed into the sea on at least three occasions. The last time was in storms on 31 January 1953, when the kitchen, scullery and two bedrooms disappeared. The walls now facing the sea are reinforced with steel rods.

3 *Captain Cook's Cottage, Church Street*

It was to this village in 1745 that James Cook came as a shop assistant. Staithes kindled in him a love of the sea which culminated in his three great voyages of exploration. The shop where Cook worked for William Sanderson was damaged by the sea, some years later, and rebuilt in Church Street. This is the house bearing a plaque known as Captain Cook's Cottage. At the end of the row of houses is Dog Laup, surely one of the narrowest thoroughfares in Britain.

4 *Murder by smugglers*

It was in the fields above Staithes in 1776 that four troopers stationed in the village tried to apprehend a group of smugglers. In the ensuing scuffle Trooper Thomas Casseldine was mortally wounded. Richard Curtis of Staithes was charged with the murder. He was brought to trial three years later and acquitted, but was still ordered to serve five years in the Royal Navy.

5 *Beacons*

At the times of the Spanish Armada and the threat of Napoleonic invasion, beacons were set on high points along the coast. If the enemy were sighted then the beacons would be lit. The flames would be seen at key beacons inland, and these would be lit in turn. The message would then be quickly passed inland to muster forces to repel the invaders. Fortunately there was no need to use the system on either occasion.

6 *Port Mulgrave*

The small harbour at the foot of the cliffs is being destroyed by the action of the sea. The harbour was built in the 1850s to take ironstone from the area to the foundries in Durham. The ore was brought to the harbour through a tunnel which is now sealed. The harbour went out of use in 1916 and the installations were removed in 1934. The houses on the cliff top were built for ironworkers and coastguards.

7 *Runswick*

In 1682 disaster struck the village when the houses slid into the sea, but fortunately no lives were lost. The new village's most prominent house—the thatched one overlooking the sea—belonged to the coastguard. With its extensive view over the bay it must have made smuggling a little more difficult. Kettleness Point at the far side of the bay has been the scene of a number of shipwrecks. In 1901 the village made history when the women launched the lifeboat. Most of their husbands were at sea when a storm broke, so with only a scratch crew of local men the boat was dragged by the women over the beach and pushed into the sea until the boat floated off its cradle—a strenuous task. The women were later invited to a dinner and reception in Manchester.

1.7

ANCIENT AND MODERN TRACKWAYS

The first half of the walk follows part of the route of the Whitby–Pickering railway, which was opened in 1836. There is an opportunity to view the workshops of the North York Moors Railway and the engines awaiting restoration. The walk continues through the wooded valley of the Murk Esk to the picturesque hamlet of Beck Hole. The return to Grosmont involves a climb onto the edge of the moors and later a walk beside an ancient paved pannierway through Crag Cliff Wood.

ROUTE DESCRIPTION (Map 7)

From the car-park turn L to the level crossing at Grosmont Station *(1)*. Turn R after the crossing through a gate signposted 'Footpath to Goathland'. Cross over a footbridge and bear L up a track which passes the church. On your R are the railway and footpath tunnels which give access to the North York Moors Railway engine sheds; the small tunnel was used by the original horse-drawn railway. Turn half R through a gate, continuing to climb, and after 50 yards (45 m) turn L through a gate (PFS). Follow the distinct track downhill keeping a wire fence on your L. Before reaching the railway line you pass a viewing area overlooking the railway's workshops *(2)*.

Pass through a gate down to the lineside and continue to a small gate which gives access to a broad track beside the line. Engines awaiting restoration are usually parked on this section of line. Continue along the side of the railway until the broad track *(3)* leaves the railway and leads into the hamlet of Esk Valley *(4)*. The track runs straight on through the wooded valley of the Murk Esk to a footbridge which crosses the river, using the original bridge pillars for support. Continuing along the track you eventually reach a few steps by the river bank, pass through the wood to a stile, and a track then leads straight on into the picturesque hamlet of Beck Hole *(5)*.

Turn L and follow the road steeply uphill. At the sharp bend there is an elevated view over the hamlet. Cross over the railway

STARTING AND FINISHING POINT
Grosmont car-park (94-825053) to the west of the A169 Whitby to Pickering road at Sleights.

LENGTH
4¾ miles (7.5 km)

ASCENT
400 feet (120 m)

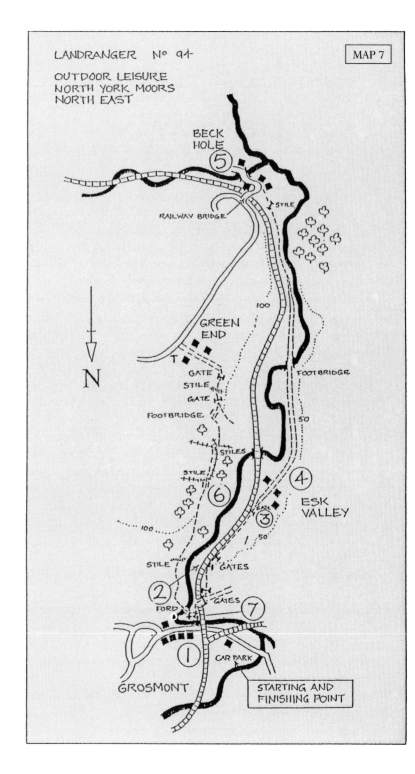

bridge and at a junction turn L along the road for ¼ mile (1.2 *Cottage at Beck Hole* km) to Green End. At the telephone box turn L down through the hamlet; at the end of the road turn R through a flagged gateway (PBS) and in 20 yards (18 m) bear L over a stile along a flagged path between walls, then continue straight on between hedges with the flagged path on the R of the farm track. Pass through a gate and immediately bear half R (PFS). The path descends to a bridge and then through open woodland. After crossing a stile into a wood, turn R to another stile into a field and turn L along the edge of the wood to a stile and footbridge into Crag Cliff Wood.

Continue along the path where you begin to see the best section of the ancient paved way *(6)*. Follow the path as people have done for centuries, pass out of the wood over a stile, and the paved way continues down the field to join a road. Turn L through a gate which crosses the road, turn L again just before

41

the ford and walk over a large footbridge. Climb the steps to the path which leads to a lane. Turn L up the lane and then R through the stile at the church (7). Continue through the churchyard and pass over a stile into the lane you departed on earlier. Turn R over the footbridge into Grosmont.

1 Grosmont

The village owes its existence to the discovery of ironstone when the railway was constructed. There were eight ironstone mines in the area and the car-park was the site of three blast furnaces which finally closed in 1915. Time and nature have mellowed all these sites.

2 North York Moors Railway

The Whitby–Pickering railway line was opened in 1836. The line was surveyed and constructed by George Stephenson, who designed the *Rocket*. Originally the coaches were pulled by horses and were shaped like a stage-coach—they carried six passengers inside, four outside in front, four behind and as many as could get on top! One horse was required to pull each carriage, with two required on the hills. On downhill sections, as from Beck Hole to Grosmont, the horses rode in dandy carts coupled to the coaches. At Goathland the carriages were drawn up an incline and reassembled to continue the journey. The line was converted to steam in 1847 and a deviation line, around the incline, was built along the present route in 1865. Under the 'Beeching Plan' the line south of Grosmont closed in 1965. The historic and scenic value of the line was recognized and a preservation society was formed. Since then volunteers and a few full-time officials have turned the line into a tourist attraction carrying over 200,000 passengers annually on both steam- and diesel-hauled trains.

3 The original railway line

Your path into Esk Valley was the original line constructed by George Stephenson. One of the sources of revenue for the line in the first few decades was stone and later iron ore; as you walk down the broad path you can see the brick-faced shaft-top of the Esk Valley Ironstone Mine on your right in a field. The mine opened in 1859 and closed some time after 1862. When it reopened in 1871 the extra shaft had to be built as a result of new laws following the New Hartley Colliery Disaster in Northumberland, when the only way into the mine was sealed as the pithead gear collapsed trapping 204 mineworkers.

Opposite *Steaming up, Grosmont*

4 *Esk Valley*

The hamlet of Esk Valley was built for workers at the nearby ironstone and whinstone mines. The first large building on the right had two upstairs floors as living quarters for four families of craftsmen at the iron mine, which was 60 yards (55 m) away on the hillside. The ground floor at the back of the building served as workshops and the mine office. The railway was the only connection with the outside world; every two weeks a train brought coal and other goods to the hamlet. When the track became unusable in 1951, the residents raised the money to construct a road to join the Goathland to Lease Rigg road.

5 *Beck Hole*

The hamlet of stone houses nestles in a hollow under the moors formed by Ellerbeck. West Beck and Ellerbeck join close to Beck Hole and form the Murk Esk. There is a fine view of the hamlet from the foot of the road to Goathland, past the inn and the bridge to the green. On summer evenings the game of quoits is played on the green as part of a local league. The players throw a metal ring weighing 5¼ pounds (2.4 kg) across an 11 yard (10 m) pitch. The idea is to throw the quoit over a metal pin—a ringer—or set the quoit against the pin to prevent your opponent getting a ringer—a gater. The pins are surrounded by a soft area in which the quoits will stick when they land. The ones on Beck Hole green are protected by square boxes.

6 *Paved ways* See page 32

7 *Grosmont Church*

The original church building was opened on 1 June 1842 to meet the needs of the expanding community, and by 1875 the present larger church had to be built. To help raise funds for the original church a three day bazaar was organized in 1839; special trains were run at reduced prices from Whitby and Pickering—these were probably the first railway excursions. Outside the west door of the church is a boulder of Shap Granite brought to the area by glacier movement.

1.8

THE HOLE OF HORCUM

This is a walk of delightful contrasts. The first mile of the route skirts the top edge of the natural hollow of the Hole of Horcum, offering fine views. The heather-covered Levisham Moor, spectacular in August, is crossed to Dundale Pond. Here the scenery changes to quiet woodland in the valleys of Dundale Griff and Levisham Beck. The return through the centre of the Hole of Horcum gives an opportunity to grasp the size and structure of this natural basin.

STARTING AND FINISHING POINT
Saltergate Bank car-park (94/100-852937) on the A169 Pickering to Whitby road.

LENGTH
5 miles (8 km)

ASCENT
600 feet (180 m)

ROUTE DESCRIPTION (Map 8)

From the large car-park cross over the road, and in front of you is the vast hollow of the Hole of Horcum *(1)*. Turn R along the track which skirts the top of the hollow and descend to join the road near the sharp bend of Saltergate Bank *(2)*. Continue straight on to a stile and gate which give access to a broad track over Levisham Moor. After a mile (1.6 km) the track descends slightly to Seavy Pond then continues through the heather for another mile to Dundale Pond *(3)*. At this pond turn L down Dundale Griff. The path down the valley continues on the R bank of the stream which quickly leaves the level moorland and cuts deeply into the tree-lined valley.

As you approach the valley bottom you pass two small valleys on your L with the quaint names of Pigtrough Griff and Water Griff, but you continue to a junction of tracks in the valley with a wooden signpost *(4)*. Turn L over the stream to a footbridge over Levisham Beck. Turn half L after crossing the bridge and continue with a wall on your R and the stream on your L. After about 300 yards (275 m) you cross over a stile and the path continues over the fields crossing two further stiles to Low Horcum Farm *(5)*. Pass the farm on your R and continue into the head of the valley. Cross over a stile, and when the stream bears L carry straight on. The path begins to climb out of the Hole of Horcum, leading into a gully up the western edge of the hollow and continuing fairly steeply up to a stile and the road on

The Hole of Horcum

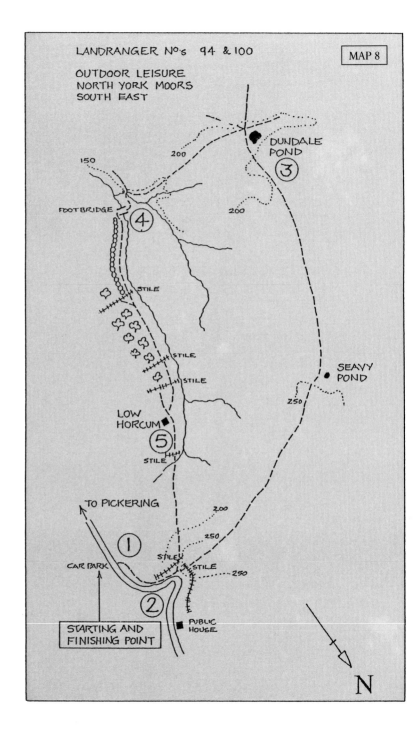

Saltergate Bank. Turn R back along the edge of the Hole of Horcum to the car-park.

1 *Hole of Horcum*

The vast hollow is a ¼ mile (1.2 km) wide slice taken out of the surrounding moorland. Legend says that Giant Wade dug the earth out of the hollow with his hand and threw it at his wife; he missed, and the hill of Blakey Topping two miles to the east was formed. The land was in fact undermined by springs many thousands of years ago and the resulting debris was washed down Levisham Beck.

2 *Saltergate Bank*

At this point on the hill there is an excellent view northwards to the Ballistic Missile Early Warning Station at RAF Fylingdales. This station gives the famous four minute warning of nuclear attack to Britain and fifteen minutes to the United States. The station also tracks satellites out in space. At the foot of the hill is the Saltergate Inn, a resting place for travellers crossing the moors. In times gone by there would be a variety of goods passing the inn, including fish from the coast, lime to sweeten the acid soils and probably contraband. Behind the inn you can see the top of Newton-dale Gorge, through which the New York Moors Railway threads its way.

3 *Dundale Pond*

This pond was probably built about 1230 when the land was given to the monks of Malton Priory as pasture for their sheep, cattle and horses. To this day common rights of Levisham Moor are owned by twenty-six local people who hold the various rights to graze over 2,000 sheep or a lesser number of cattle; the Right of Turbary (to collect turf for fires); the right of estovers (to collect wood); the right of piscary (to fish) and also the right to graze a limited amount of poultry and horses.

4 *Levisham Beck Woods*

The woods support a wide variety of birds. If you are lucky you may see tits, treecreepers, woodpeckers, blackcaps or a dipper winging its way just above the stream.

5 *Horcum*

The land at the bottom of the Hole of Horcum supported two farms up to about twenty years ago. The one at Low Horcum has been restored, but High Horcum, at the northern end of the hollow, has now disappeared.

2.9

OSMOTHERLEY AND THE DROVE ROAD

STARTING AND
FINISHING POINT
Sheepwash car-
park (100-469993).
Turn east off A19
Thirsk to
Middlesbrough
road to
Osmotherley. Turn
L in village on
Swainby road for
1½ miles (2.5 km).

LENGTH
6 miles (9.5 km)

ASCENT
450 feet (140 m)

The Scottish drovers bringing their cattle south to the English markets in the eighteenth and nineteenth centuries used the ancient Hambleton Street. This clearly defined walk sets out on this track and then follows a woodland path leading across to the attractive village of Osmotherley. Here the Cleveland Way is joined for a circuit of Scarth Wood Moor, revealing extensive views to the west and north.

ROUTE DESCRIPTION (Map 9)

From the car-park turn R up the road towards Swainby. When the road turns L turn R over a footbridge and follow the broad track up a short hill (1) continuing south alongside a plantation. After ¼ mile (1.2 km) turn R over a stile beside a gate with a fenced pond on your L. Walk down the broad ride between the trees crossing two other rides, pass a ruined building on your R then cross a lane to a gate. The track descends between trees following a stream on your L. Pass the ruins of Cote Garth on your R. Continue on the track to a gate which leads down to a tarmac road, turn R past the Youth Hostel and climb up to a junction. When you reach the junction, turn L down the road into Osmotherley (2).

Return back up the road towards Swainby and turn L along Ruebury Lane, where there is a Cleveland Way signpost (3). As the road swings R a fine view opens up across the plain below. There is an indicator pointing out places to be seen at the fork in the tracks. Your route lies to the L, but the track on the R leads up to the Lady Chapel (4) ¼ mile (1.2 km) away, a diversion well worth undertaking, returning to this point.

Continue on the broad track, pass Chapel Wood Farm on your L, and continue through two gates into a wood. Fork R on the Cleveland Way track which climbs steadily through the trees. At the top follow a stone wall on your R. Pass a GPO booster station screened by the woods, and a short while later you pass an OS obelisk on your R just over the wall (5). Pass

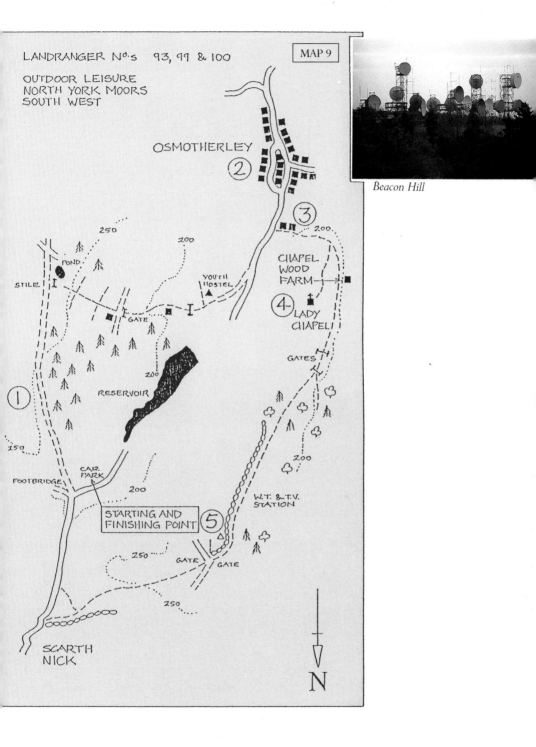

OUTDOOR LEISURE
NORTH YORK MOORS
SOUTH WEST

Beacon Hill

OSMOTHERLEY
②

250

200

③   200.

POND

STILE

YOUTH
HOSTEL

CHAPEL
WOOD
FARM

GATE

④ LADY
CHAPEL

200

GATES

RESERVOIR

200

①

150

② 200

CAR.
PARK

W.T. & T.V.
STATION

FOOTBRIDGE

200

STARTING AND
FINISHING POINT ⑤

250

GATE   GATE

250

SCARTH
NICK

N

through two gates and follow the broad track across the moor.
The finest views are now to the north across the Cleveland
Plain. The path eventually joins a wall descending to the road in
Scarth Nick. Turn R along the road back to the car-park.

1 *The Hambleton Drove Road*

The ancient trackway became popular with Scottish drovers bringing their cattle south, on the hoof, to sell at the English markets. The trade reached its peak in the early nineteenth century before the railways took over the trade. The route climbed through Scarth Nick then passed the Chequers Inn and over Black Hambleton. It then split near Steeple Cross, one road continuing south to York while a south-eastern road led down Stocking Lane to Malton, continuing south over the Wolds and River Humber into Lincolnshire and Norfolk.

2 *Osmotherley*

This attractive village of stone houses stands on the edge of the moors overlooking the plain. In the centre of the village is the market cross and a stone table set on five short stone legs where produce for sale could be displayed. Fish was sold here as late as 1874. The church stands on the site of a Saxon church, but the earliest part of the present building is the Norman south doorway.

3 *The Cleveland Way*

The 112 miles (180 km) Long Distance Footpath starts at Helmsley and heads west to Sutton Bank and Kilburn White Horse. The route then turns north to Osmotherley, over the Cleveland Hills and Roseberry Topping to the coast at Saltburn. For the last fifty-two miles (84 km) the cliff top path is followed, passing through Whitby and Scarborough to finish at Filey Brigg.

4 *The Lady Chapel*

The small chapel is attached to a stone house set amidst trees. It was reputedly built in 1515 by Queen Katherine of Aragon, first wife of Henry VIII, for the recluse Thomas Parkinson.

5 *Scarth Wood Moor OS obelisk*

This is one end of the Lyke Wake Walk, the other end of the forty miles (64 km) moorland walk being Beacon Howe, above Ravenscar, on the coast. The route was devised by Bill Cowley and first walked in October 1955 by him and twelve other walkers. At peak weekends in the early 1980s over a thousand people at a time were completing the challenge. The track over the high moors is now very eroded, and large groups are being advised against undertaking the walk to give the path a chance to recover.

Scarth Wood Moor

2.10

HACKNESS AND WHISPERDALES

STARTING AND
FINISHING POINT
Reasty Bank car-
park (94/101-
964943).
Turn south off the
A171 Scarborough
to Whitby road,
north of the Falcon
Inn, towards
Harwood Dale.
Turn R just before
the village to
Hackness. The car-
park is at the top of
the steep hill.

LENGTH
7½ miles (12 km)

ASCENT
450 feet (140 m)

The early part of the walk is through a conifer plantation, then across farmland. The descent to Hackness is through a deciduous wood rich in wild flowers in summer. The picturesque village of Hackness was the site of a convent established in the seventh century by St Hilda of Whitby, and there are parts of an Anglian cross in the church. The return is along peaceful Whisperdales with valley fields overlooked by conifer-topped heights.

ROUTE DESCRIPTION (Map 10)

From the car-park on the eastern side of the road take the track which keeps to the top of the plateau—not the one marked with a PFS. There are views over Harwood Dale from the car-park. The track passes beneath the trees. After 600 yards (550 m) a path on your L leads in 50 yards (45 m) to a fine view-point over the fields to Scarborough Castle, but your route carries straight on along the plateau top. Eventually the track swings R to a road; cross the road coming in from your L and continue along the roadside for 50 yards (45 m) then turn L at a PFS. This narrower but still distinct track passes in a semi-circle beneath the trees to join the road further south. Turn R parallel with the road and turn L at the road junction to Silpho.

At the end of the wood pass Thieves Dikes and 200 yards (180 m) later turn L at the PFS. Cross two fields keeping the hedge on your R. Turn L at the PFS along the edge of a field, then R at the next PFS along the edge of fields with a stone wall on your R. After crossing two stiles turn R to a stile and descend into a valley. Turn L down the valley (PFS to Hackness) and pass over a stile into a wood. The hillside track leads through the deciduous wood which has a wide variety of wild flowers (1). On reaching the road descend the steep hill to a T-junction in Hackness. Your route lies to the R but you may wish to turn L and visit the church first (2).

Having turned R, you turn R again after 100 yards (90m)

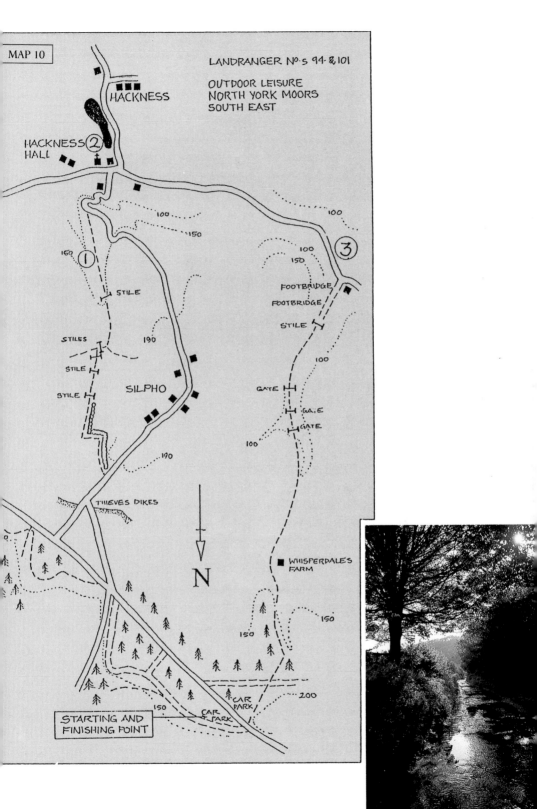

MAP 10

LANDRANGER Nº·s 94·& 101

OUTDOOR LEISURE
NORTH YORK MOORS
SOUTH EAST

HACKNESS

HACKNESS ②
HALL

100
150
160 ①
100
100
STILE
150
③
FOOTBRIDGE
FOOTBRIDGE
STILE
STILES
190
100
STILE
STILE
SILPHO
GATE
GATE
GATE
100
190
100
THIEVES DIKES

N

WHISPERDALES
FARM

150
150
150
200
CAR PARK
CAR PARK

STARTING AND
FINISHING POINT
150

Low Dales Ford

along the road signposted 'Low Dales and High Dales only'. This lane leads through the quiet pastoral valley for a mile (1.6 km); you may then encounter a flooded road *(3)*, so fork R over the footbridge and stile and follow the hedge on your L to Low Dales, walking parallel with the road.

At the fork in the road bear R, cross a footbridge over a stream, fork R again to another footbridge and then a stile. The track leads up the valley passing through gates and over stiles and then swings R around Whisperdales Farm; it then climbs steadily into a forest and sweeps R. At the next junction you can see a boundary marker inscribed 'SIL'; continue on your track back to the car-park at Reasty Bank.

1 *Hilda Wood*

The wood probably takes its name from St Hilda, the Abbess of Whitby Abbey who founded a cell of the Celtic abbey at Hackness. On a walk through the woods in the late spring you should find an interesting selection of wild flowers beside the path, including wood anemone, red campion, forget-me-not, wild garlic, bluebell, lesser celandine and primrose.

2 *Hackness Church*

The church stands on the site of a Celtic cell set up by Whitby Abbey. Begu, one of the nuns, saw the death of St Hilda in a dream and informed the other nuns hours before the news arrived from Whitby. A Benedictine house was founded on the site in the eleventh century. The present church on the same site contains a late Saxon chancel arch and some Norman work. Inside the church are two pieces of an Anglo-Saxon cross.

3 *Low Dales Ford*

This section of road is often flooded and must be the longest ford in Yorkshire.

Autumn in Hilda Wood

2.11

A SHIPWRECK TRAIL

STARTING POINT
Lifeboat Museum,
Whitby (94-
898114).

FINISHING POINT
The Dock, Robin
Hood's Bay (94-
953048).

LENGTH
7 miles (11 km)

ASCENT
500 feet (150 m)

The Lifeboat Museum in Whitby contains one of the last rowing lifeboats and items from numerous wrecks along this stretch of coast. Many lives have been lost, but given a fighting chance these local people would wrestle victory from disaster. The walk keeps to the cliff-top path with easy route-finding and fine views. The walk ends in the interesting village of Robin Hood's Bay with its crowded collection of stone cottages.

ROUTE DESCRIPTION (Maps 11, 12)

From the Lifeboat Museum turn R upstream and cross the swing bridge over the River Esk. Take the second turn L along Church Street to the 199 Steps (1). Ascend the steps passing Caedmon Cross (2) at the top to the parish church (3). Continue on, out of the churchyard, to a car-park with Whitby Abbey (4) on your R. Turn L across the car-park and head for the base of the television transmitter. A path passes it on the seaward side and continues south along the cliff-top path.

As you approach Saltwick Nab you pass the scene of the *Rohilla* disaster (5), which brought about acts of heroism rarely surpassed. The path leads into a holiday village. Continue on the road between the buildings and pick up the cliff-top path just beyond the entrance to the site. To the L is a rock tooth sticking out of the sea. This was the site of one of the most recent wrecks, when the Scarborough fishing boat *Admiral Von Tromp* ran ashore. The path passes on the seaward side of the former Whitby fog horn, then passes inland around the lighthouse and afterwards rejoins the cliff-top path.

Continue south on the cliff top (6) to North Cheek. The Cheek was the scene of the shipwreck of the *Heatherfield* (7). From this point Robin Hood's Bay begins to open out but Bay Town remains hidden until the last moment. Eventually turn R at a small gate PFS, cross a short footbridge, and you are soon passing houses and entering Mount Pleasant North. At the end of the road turn L down to the car-park on the cliff top. As you

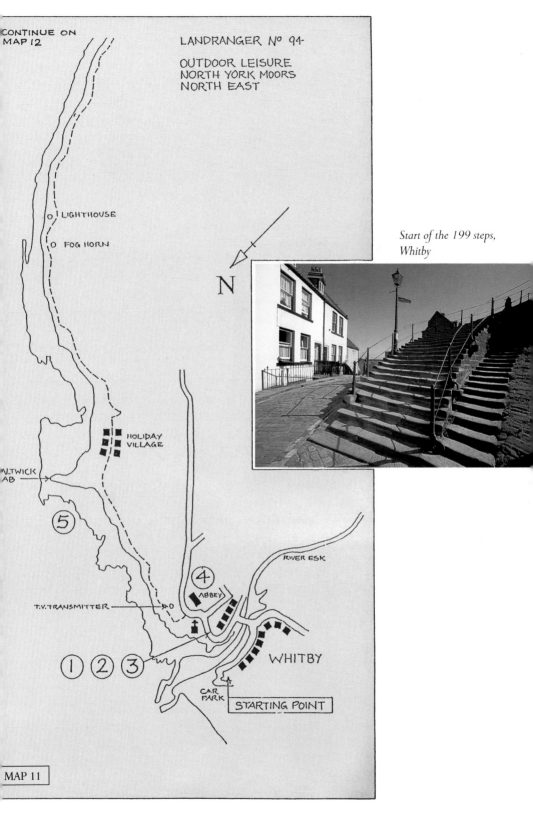

LANDRANGER Nº 94

OUTDOOR LEISURE
NORTH YORK MOORS
NORTH EAST

O LIGHTHOUSE

O FOG HORN

N

*Start of the 199 steps,
Whitby*

HOLIDAY
VILLAGE

N.TWICK
AB

⑤

RIVER ESK

④ ABBEY

T.V. TRANSMITTER ——— P.O

① ② ③

WHITBY

CAR
PARK

STARTING POINT

MAP 11

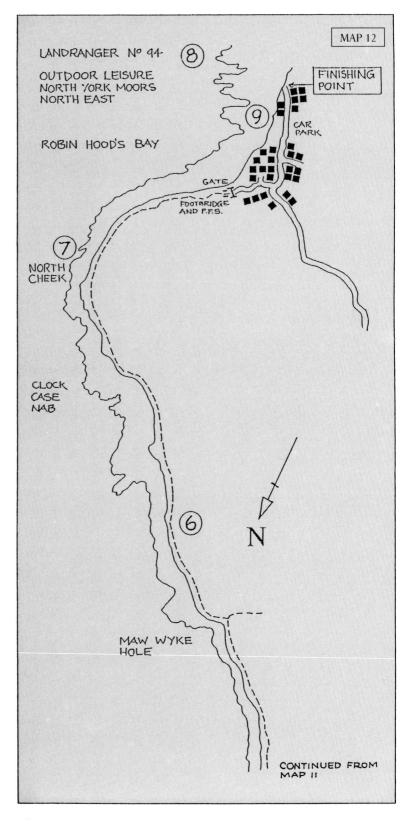

MAP 12

LANDRANGER N° 94

⑧

OUTDOOR LEISURE
NORTH YORK MOORS
NORTH EAST

FINISHING
POINT

⑨

CAR
PARK

ROBIN HOOD'S BAY

GATE

FOOTBRIDGE
AND P.F.S.

⑦

NORTH
CHEEK

CLOCK
CASE
NAB

⑥

N

MAW WYKE
HOLE

CONTINUED FROM
MAP 11

begin to descend into the village you have a fine view over the house-tops into Robin Hood's Bay *(8)*. The road descends steeply into Bay Town turning R at the Laurel Inn, then turn L after the bridge to reach the slipway down to the beach. You have to return to the car-park at the top of the cliff for transport, but explore the many passageways in this interesting village *(9)* on the way back.

1 *199 steps*
   Count them—they have been worn over the years by people climbing to their cliff-top church. To the right of the steps is the old cobbled carriageway for horsedrawn traffic to Abbey House.

2 *Caedmon Cross*
   The 20 feet (6 m) sandstone cross commemorates Caedmon, a lay brother at Whitby Abbey. After a dream he began to compose sacred verse and is acknowledged as the father of English sacred music.

Whitby Parish Church

3 *Whitby parish church*
   The church has an interesting and unusual interior. It still contains box pews, some bearing the names of nearby villages who used them. Beside the pulpit is an ear trumpet for the use of a former minister's deaf wife. The interior was built in 1612 by local shipwrights and resembles the interior of a ship.

4 *Whitby Abbey*
   The original abbey on this site was the setting for the Synod of Whitby in 664, which fixed the date of Easter. The present ruins are in the Early English style with a few Decorated windows. The nave collapsed during a storm in 1763 and the central tower in 1830. Further damage was sustained during the bombardment of Whitby by German warships in 1914.

5 *The* Rohilla *disaster*
   On 30 October 1914 the hospital ship *Rohilla* was believed to have struck a mine and ran aground on Saltwick Nab with 229 people on board. The Whitby lifeboat couldn't be rowed out of the harbour due to a gale, so they dragged it on its carriage along the foot of the cliffs and launched it near the wreck. At the first attempt they rescued seventeen people. The lifeboat was swept along the coast, but it was dragged back for a second attempt and eighteen lives were saved. The lifeboat was then smashed against the cliffs by the rising tide. The Upgang lifeboat was lowered down the cliff but the high tide prevented the boat from being launched. A tug from

Hartlepool attempted to get Whitby's second lifeboat to the scene but failed. Teesmouth's motor lifeboat was summoned but was disabled and had to return to port. Scarborough's lifeboat was towed to the scene by a tug, but due to the storm and after sixteen hours at sea the exhausted crew failed to get close. Eventually the Tynemouth motor lifeboat battled forty-four miles (71 km) down the coast and managed to get alongside. In fifty hours, with the use of six lifeboats, they had saved 85 lives, and a further sixty people had been washed ashore alive. The RNLI issued three gold medals and four silver medals for outstanding heroism.

6 *The Cleveland Way and Coast to Coast Walk*
The whole walk is along part of the Cleveland Way (see Route 9). At Maw Wyke Hole the path is used by walkers on Alfred Wainwright's Coast to Coast Walk. They are at the end of a 190 miles (306 km) walk from St Bees Head in Cumbria to Robin Hood's Bay.

7 Heatherfield *shipwreck*
On 26 January 1936 the 500-ton (492-tonne) coaster *Heatherfield* ran ashore on North Cheek in fog. The rocket brigade fired lines from the cliff top and the second shot straddled the ship 200 yards (180 m) off shore. The crew were taken off by breeches buoy.

8 *The* Visitor *shipwreck*
The bay was the scene of a dramatic rescue in 1881 of the crew of the brig *Visitor*. At 8.00 a.m. on 18 January the people of Bay Town witnessed the sinking of the ship. Six of the crew had taken to a boat and were sheltering from the storm in the lee of the wreck. The Whitby lifeboat couldn't get out of the harbour due to the storm so it was decided to take it to the bay by land. The roads were covered up to a depth of seven feet (2 m) in snow but sixty men started digging through the drifts from Whitby while folk from Bay Town started digging to meet them. Eleven horses and 200 men manhandled the boat out of Whitby and over the moor top. The lifeboat was lowered into the village, passing the corner at the Laurel Inn with only inches to spare, to be launched to the wreck. At the first attempt the furious sea smashed six oars, at the second attempt a crew of eighteen battled through the storm to rescue the survivors.

9 *Robin Hood's Bay and smuggling* See page 37.

Looking across Whitby harbour

2.12

THE PACKHORSE TRACKS OF COMMONDALE MOOR

STARTING AND
FINISHING POINT
Commondale
village (94-662104).
Turn south off the
A171 Whitby to
Guisborough road
towards Castleton.
After 2½ miles
(4 km) turn R to
Commondale.

LENGTH
7 miles (11 km)

ASCENT
600 feet (180 m)

The moorlands are crossed by many ancient paved tracks and this walk incorporates a number of these. This is an excellent moorland walk, with views of the sea from the high points. One part of the route is poorly defined and some easy compass work may need to be undertaken to reach Hob Cross. For this reason, it would be better walked on a fine day.

ROUTE DESCRIPTION (Maps 13, 14)

From the village walk up the road towards Kildale and Stokesley. Pass the 'Commondale' village sign and 100 yards (90 m) later turn R along a track near a group of trees. Turn R at the PFS to Guisborough and a grassy track crosses open moorland and joins a short section of paved way *(1)*. Fork R shortly after joining the paved way, cross the moorland stream and the track climbs up the hillside and eventually joins a broader track. Continue straight ahead and in 50 yards (45 m) fork L on a track to a memorial *(2)*.

Rejoin the broad track, then follow a bearing of 352° magnetic, keeping a line of grouse butts on your L to reach a stone pillar inscribed 'Hob on the Hill' *(3)*. Then take a compass reading of 10° magnetic for ¼ mile (1.2 km) to Hob Cross, a stone with that inscription set on a mound. It stands on the moor about 100 yards (90 m) short of a stone wall. There are fine views over the moorlands to the coastline and sea beyond.

Turn R at Hob Cross on a narrow track marked with wooden posts with blue arrows. Cross under the overhead wires and continue to the paved Quaker Path. Turn half R along this fine exposed section of causeway, and when it ends continue along the path to the road. Lockwood Beck reservoir comes into view on your L. Turn R along the road.

At the first bend you can shorten the route by following a line of boundary stones across the moor; keep to the L of the wood and turn half R down the road into Commondale.

For the main route continue on the unfenced moorland road

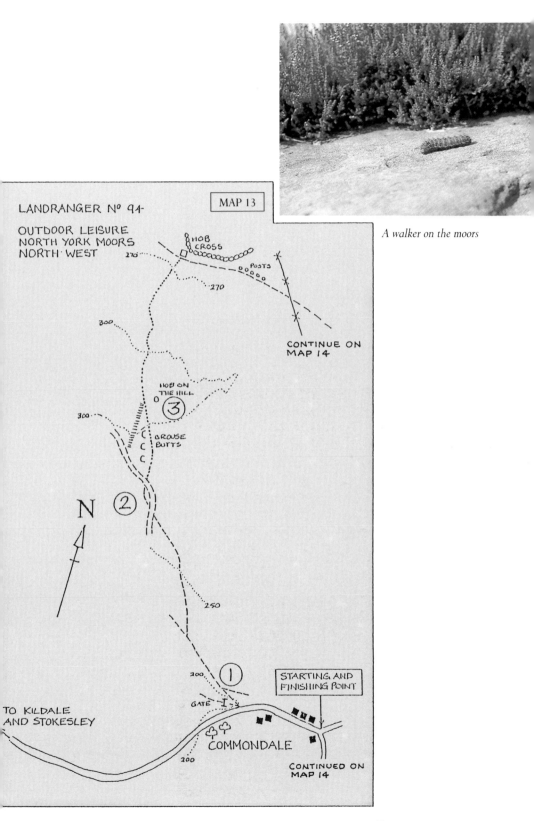

LANDRANGER Nº 94-

OUTDOOR LEISURE
NORTH YORK MOORS
NORTH WEST

MAP 13

HOB
CROSS

270

POSTS

270

300

CONTINUE ON
MAP 14

HOB ON
THE HILL

③

300

GROUSE
BUTTS

N

②

250

200

①

STARTING AND
FINISHING POINT

GATE

TO KILDALE
AND STOKESLEY

COMMONDALE

200

CONTINUED ON
MAP 14

A walker on the moors

65

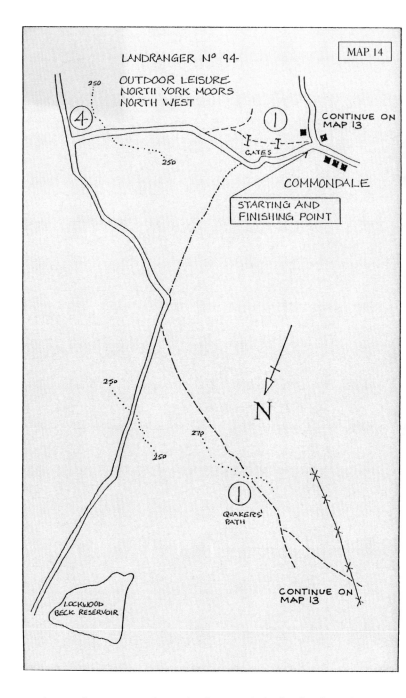

to the road junction where the base and shaft of White Cross *(4)* is situated. Turn R down the road towards Commondale and at the bend in the road bear L onto the paved way, turning half R along it towards Commondale. Short sections of the paved way *(1)* are missing, but the line of the route continues to a gate

Opposite *Hob on the Hill*

and then crosses two fields. Here the paving is covered with grass, arriving at the crossroads in Commondale where you started.

The War Memorial, Commondale Moor

1 *Paved Ways* See page 32.

2 *War memorial*
The stone is a memorial to Guardsmen Robbie Leggott, who was killed in action in 1916, and Alf Cockerill, who died of wounds received during the First World War. It was erected by Hon. Margaret Bruce Challoner in the area where these two volunteers had spent their boyhood, one of them shepherding his father's flock.

3 *Hobs*
These were local folklore characters which were thought to be something similar to elves. Some were mischievous and others were helpful to the farmers. They were associated with various places on the moor and at least twenty-four were recorded by George Calvert in a manuscript written in 1823.

4 *White Cross*
This White Cross should not be confused with the White Cross known as Fat Betty at the head of Rosedale. The stone base and shaft stand on the old moorland road from Whitby. At this point the road may have split, one route going down the side of the Leven Valley to Stokesley, while a north-western route went along the Quaker Path to Guisborough.

2.13

THE LEVISHAM CIRCUIT

The moorland village of Levisham stands on a plateau. The first part of the walk is through wooded Newtondale, close to the North York Moors Railway. A solitary church is passed on the way to Levisham, then the walk continues over the moor to Skelton Tower, with its excellent viewpoint overlooking Newtondale. The paths throughout the walk are obvious.

ROUTE DESCRIPTION (Map 15)

From the car-park on the bend, walk up the road towards Levisham. After 150 yards (140 m) bear R on a footpath (PFS), then fork L almost immediately along the moorland edge above the fields. Eventually the path swings L around the hillside and passes through a gate into a conifer wood. The path descends to the R and continues down the valley, keeping the railway line *(1)* about 100 yards (90 m) away on your R.

The walk continues south through West Bank Wood and the path may be wet at times. As you approach Farwath *(2)* you come closer to the railway line. Pass through a gate and skirt the woodland, cross over a wire-fenced stream at the bridge and continue to a gate, turn back half L at the gate away from the ford, do not go through the gate, pass over a bridge and keep to the L of the field. Pass through the edge of Hagg Wood Reserve, belonging to the Yorkshire Naturalists' Trust. Take the second path that gently climbs the hillside. It is a good path which levels out and continues along the hillside to join the road on Levisham Bank. As you approach the road you pass the solitary church *(3)* on your R.

Turn L up the road into Levisham village—beware of the traffic. Pass through the village of stone cottages set on either side of the green, then take the road to the R of the inn. As you approach the gate at the end of this moor road the Hole of Horcum *(4)* comes into view in the distance on the R. Pass over the stile (PFS) and follow the track across the moor to Dundale Pond *(5)*. Turn half L in front of the pond up a small valley.

STARTING AND
FINISHING POINT
Above Levisham
Station (94/100-
820916).
Turn west off the
A169 Pickering to
Whitby road to
Lockton and
Levisham, fork L at
the top of the
village to Levisham
Station, after 1¼
miles (2 km) park
on moor at sharp
bend.

LENGTH
7½ miles (12 km)

ASCENT 550 feet
(170 m)

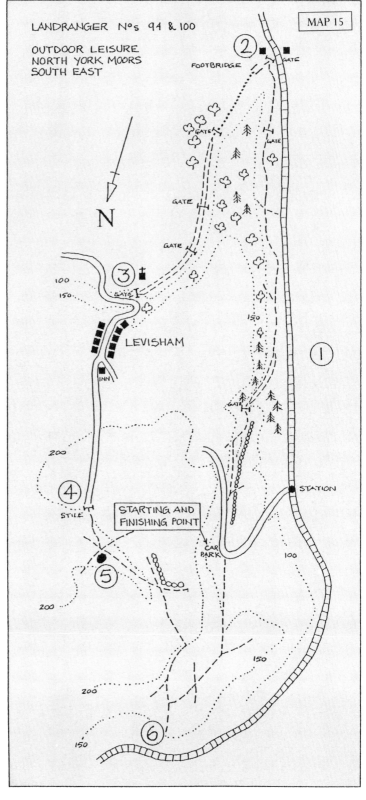

LANDRANGER Nos 94 & 100

OUTDOOR LEISURE
NORTH YORK MOORS
SOUTH EAST

MAP 15

N

FOOTBRIDGE

GATE

LEVISHAM

INN

STARTING AND
FINISHING POINT

STILE

STATION

CAR
PARK

Opposite *Skelton Tower*

After 100 yards (90 m) the path rises to a wall corner; bear half R across the open moor to a viewpoint on the ridge. Below is the track going to the L which will take you back to the start, and on the R is ruined Skelton Tower. Turn R down the hillside on the track and cross the open moor to Skelton Tower *(6)*. Return 100 yards (90 m) to a junction and then turn R along the track back to the car-park.

Weather vane, Levisham

1 *North York Moors Railway* See page 42.
2 *Farwath*
   This remote hamlet is one of the last places in the area where besoms are made. These are the heather brooms which are still sold in a few of the shops in the area. At the turn of this century it was a large cottage industry, the besoms being sold to dealers in Pickering who transported many of them to the shipyards. They were used in their thousands to skim slag off molten metal.
3 *St Mary's Church*
   The church stands in the wooded valley, looking sadly neglected. The original church was probably built on the site at about the time of the Norman Conquest, to serve both Lockton and Levisham. The church was largely rebuilt in 1804 and restored in 1897.
4 *The Hole of Horcum* See page 49.
5 *Dundale Pond* See page 49.
6 *Skelton Tower*
   The ruined building was built as a shooting lodge and retreat. From the tower site there is an excellent view down into wooded Newtondale, with the North York Moors Railway threading its way through the steep-sided gorge.

2·14

THE CLEVELAND HILLS

From the Cleveland Plain the line of hills south of Stokesley beckon the walker to the North York Moors. Running from east to west are Hasty Bank, Cold Moor, Cringle Moor and Carlton Bank. Each hill offers at least 400 feet (120 m) of climbing to reach the summit, and all four hills offer excellent view-points. This walk visits the summits of the first three of these hills, returning on an old jet miners' track.

ROUTE DESCRIPTION (Map 16)

From the car-park turn L up the road, and at the top turn R up a series of steps. Cross over the ladder stile and continue on the path which winds up to the top of the hill *(1)*. On reaching the top you have an excellent view, south into Bilsdale and north over the Cleveland Plain to Roseberry Topping. The ridge path keeps to the northern edge of the hill, finally descending among the crags of the Wainstones *(2)* into a col.

Climb again, passing through a gate, to the summit of Cold Moor. Descend on the path to a gate. The walk then continues with a wall on the R turning R to a gate. Turn L beyond the gate

STARTING AND
FINISHING POINT
Clay Bank car-park
(93-572035) on the
B1257 Helmsley to
Stokesley road.

LENGTH
7 miles (11 km)

ASCENT
1300 feet (400 m)

*The jet miners' track,
Cringle Moor*

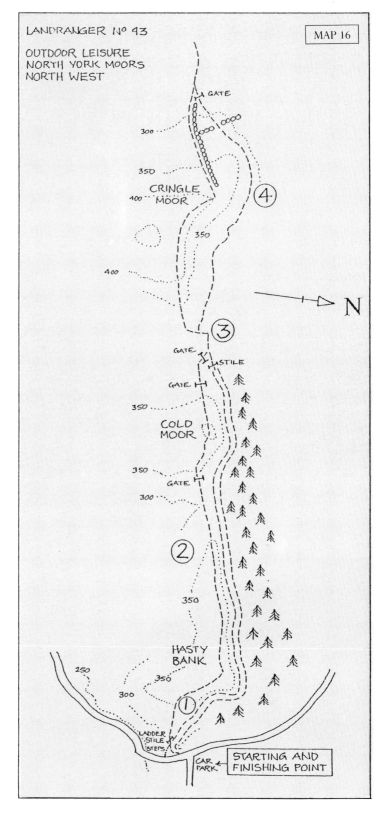

GATE

300

350

CRINGLE
MOOR

400

350

400

③

④

GATE

STILE

GATE

350

COLD
MOOR

350

GATE

300

②

350

HASTY
BANK

250

350

300

①

LADDER
STILE
STEPS

CAR
PARK

STARTING AND
FINISHING POINT

N

Opposite *The
Cleveland Plain*

along the track *(3)* and begin the ascent of Cringle Moor, the highest of the hills. The path keeps to the northern edge with the sheer cliff face tumbling away to the Cleveland Plain far below. Here, as on Hasty Bank, you have the feel of the mountains.

The path passes below the summit but visits Cringle End, an excellent view-point with a view indicator and stone seat. With an extensive panorama spread out before you this is a fine place to take a break. Continue descending the western slope of Cringle Moor with a wall on your R. When it ends turn half back R through a gate and continue on the track which passes through a gap in a stone wall.

The distinct track *(4)* contours around the northern side of Cringle Moor, giving a view of the steep cliffs. For a short while you rejoin the path you came on earlier between Cold Moor and Cringle Moor, cross two small streams and pass over a stile. The broad track, which can be muddy at times, continues for 2 miles (3 km) above the forest. When the track swings L downhill, near a seat, carry straight on past the stile you crossed earlier and descend the steps to the road. Turn L back to the car-park.

1 Jet mining

Looking along the hillside you can see a line of shale heaps removed from the hill in the search for the elusive jet. A miner could spend weeks digging into the hillside in various places and find nothing—others would strike a lucky pocket of jet and have their efforts repaid many times over. The jet trade boomed in the 1870s around Whitby where many workshops turned out extremely fine jewellery. The rough jet would be sold to dealers who came out from Whitby to purchase stock. See page 97.

2 The Wainstones

This series of rock outcrops pierce the skyline when viewed from certain places in Bilsdale and Cleveland. There are a number of rock climbs on the faces, and it is usual to see someone climbing if you visit the outcrops at a weekend.

3 Donna Cross

Close to the wall in the col between Cold Moor and Cringle Moor is the socket stone that carried Donna Cross. This cross marked the route from Kirkby into Bilsdale.

4 The jet miners' track

This old track around the side of the hills was used by jet workers. In recent years it has become a bad weather route for walkers on the Lyke Wake Walk and Cleveland Way.

2·15

THE CAPTAIN COOK CIRCUIT

The walk starts from Great Ayton, where James Cook, the explorer, spent his childhood. The walk then climbs, steeply in places, to the summit of Easby Moor, where there is a monument to Cook. There are extensive views, including the peak of Roseberry Topping. After a moorland walk you ascend this fine view-point. The return to Great Ayton is made past Airy Holme Farm, where James Cook lived and his father worked.

STARTING AND FINISHING POINT
The Captain Cook Museum, Great Ayton (93-561107).

LENGTH
7½ miles (12 km)

ASCENT
1350 feet (410 m)

ROUTE DESCRIPTION (Maps 17, 18)

From the Captain Cook Museum *(1)* in Great Ayton, cross the road, turn R and cross over the footbridge. Fork L on the path by the weir to a gate. Bear half L along the distinct path, cross a stile and continue past a sports field on your R. The track bears half L across two fields, with the Cook Monument on the skyline, to a footbridge and a path that leads to a road. Turn R along the road into Little Ayton, turning L just before the bridge.

Walk up the road, pass through a gate, then skirt L around the farm buildings. Fork L up a broad track which crosses over a railway line. Continue to a T-junction, where you then turn R along a lane which rises steadily for ½ mile (800 m). When you reach the corner of a stone wall on your L turn L up to a gate into a forest. Turn half R and follow the path steeply up into the trees. Cross straight over a forest road and continue climbing with extensive views unfolding over the Cleveland Plain. As you reach the top and leave the trees the Captain Cook Monument *(2)* comes into view. On approaching the monument note the path on your L—this is your route of descent.

The view from the monument on a fine day extends to Marton, now part of Middlesbrough, where James Cook was born in 1728. Take the path across the moor you noted on your approach and continue down some steps; the path eventually becomes a broad track between the trees. When you reach the

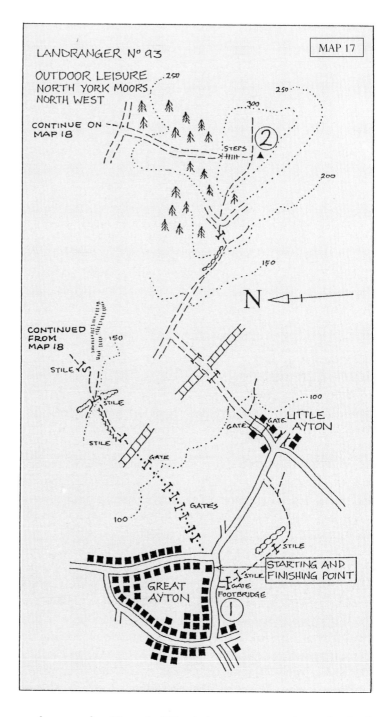

MAP 17

LANDRANGER Nº 93

OUTDOOR LEISURE
NORTH YORK MOORS,
NORTH WEST

CONTINUE ON
MAP 18

CONTINUED
FROM
MAP 18

STILE

STILE

STILE

STEPS

N

GATE

LITTLE
AYTON

GATE

STILE

GATE

GATES

STILE

STARTING AND
FINISHING POINT

GREAT
AYTON

STILE
GATE
FOOTBRIDGE

road turn R for 50 yards (45 m) then turn L on the path which
climbs to Great Ayton Moor (Cleveland Way sign) *(3)*. Climb
the steps leading up beside the old stone wall and continue
along the edge of the moor with a stone wall on your L. Pass
through a gate, cross the col and climb steeply to the summit of
Roseberry Topping *(4)*.

78

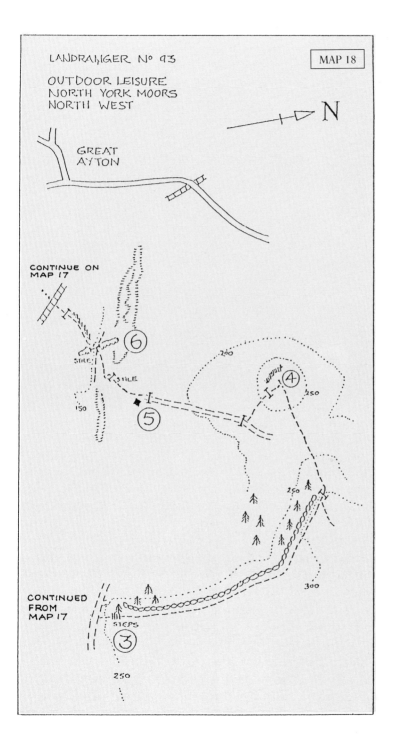

Captain Cook's school, Great Ayton

Be careful of your route of descent—there is a sheer cliff. Retrace your steps from the summit for 30 yards (25 m) and turn R down the hillside to a gate; walk down the field to join a track and turn R through a gate. Follow the track to Airy Holme Farm *(5)*. Turn R over a cattle grid (PFS) then half L across a field to a stile to the L of a group of conifers. Turn L between the wire fences. There is a steep drop on your R where mining has taken place *(6)*. In 50 yards (45 m) turn R down a hillside; this is covered in bluebells each year in the late spring. Cross a track near a metal gate, descending to a stile, and after 20 yards (18 m) turn R alongside a wire fence to another stile.

Carry straight on with a hedge on your R, cross over a railway line and continue down the field through parkland. The path goes in a straight line passing through a number of metal gates until it reaches a road in Great Ayton. Turn L along the road, taking the second turn R back to the Captain Cook Museum.

Roseberry Topping from Easby Moor

1 *Captain Cook Museum*

The building was built in 1704 as a school at the expense of a local yeoman named Michael Postgate. It was to this school that James Cook came from nearby Airy Holme Farm. The cost of Cook's education was probably borne by Thomas Scottowe, Lord of the Manor of Ayton, who employed Cook's father as a hind or foreman. The school was rebuilt in 1785 and now contains a Cook Museum.

2 *Captain Cook Monument*

The monument, erected by Robert Campion of nearby Easby Hall, overlooks Marton where the explorer was born and Great Ayton where he spent his childhood. The 51 foot (15.5 m) high memorial was completed on the centenary of Cook's birth on 27 October 1827. There is an inscription on three cast-iron panels on the monument.

3 *The Cleveland Way* See page 53.

4 *Roseberry Topping*

The hill offers an extremely fine view over Middlesbrough and along the coast. The steep crag to the west of the hill appeared when iron workings driven into the hill collapsed. The hill is close to where James Cook spent his boyhood and there is little doubt that someone as adventurous as Cook would have climbed this peak—probably gaining his first sight of the sea.

5 *Airy Holme Farm*

When James Cook was about seven his father moved from Marton to Airy Holme Farm to work as hind for Thomas Scottowe. When Cook's father retired he built a stone cottage in Great Ayton, beside the road to Easby. The cottage was shipped to Australia in 1933 and now stands in Fitzroy Gardens, Melbourne. An obelisk of stones from Point Hicks Hill, the first part of Australia sighted by Captain Cook, now stands on the site of the cottage.

6 *Whinstone mining*

Cutting across the North York Moors from a point north-east of Goathland to a point north of Great Ayton is the Cleveland Dyke. This narrow band of volcanic rock welled up out of the earth and solidified. As it is extremely hard, the whinstone has been quarried and used for surfacing roads.

2·16

THE SCENERY OF ROBIN HOOD'S BAY

This walk offers some excellent views into Robin Hood's Bay, an area of interest to the geologist. A steep climb is made through the picturesque fishermen's houses of Bay Town and an easy return is made along the former track of the Scarborough–Whitby Railway. The surrounding woodlands may reveal a wide range of birds.

STARTING AND FINISHING POINT
Ravenscar car-park (94-980014).
Turn east off the A171 Scarborough to Whitby road.

LENGTH
8½ miles (14 km)

ASCENT
1000 feet (300 m)

ROUTE DESCRIPTION (Maps 19, 20)

From the car-park walk down the road towards the Raven Hall Hotel. There is an excellent view over the fields into Robin Hood's Bay. Turn L at the entrance to the hotel down the broad path which passes the National Trust Information Centre. You pass a sign indicating 'trail' to your L—this is the route on which you will return. After ¼ mile (400 m) fork R at a National Trust sign; the route you are walking is part of the Cleveland Way (1), and you may find occasional signs indicating the route. Continue downhill and when the track joins another from the R bear L on the path to Robin Hood's Bay.

Pass over a stile and fork half R at a Cleveland Way sign. Cross the field to a stile and continue with a hedge on your L to another stile. Turn R down the field keeping a wire fence on your R to a stile onto the cliff-top path. Turn L, and there is a fine view around the bay including the village of Robin Hood's Bay (2), known locally as Bay Town. Continue on the cliff-top path, pass a World War II pill box and eventually join the road. Turn R along the road, which eventually descends very steeply (3) to the beach.

Cross over the footbridge and climb the steps back to the cliff-top path. Eventually the path descends to Boggle Hole Youth Hostel (4). When you reach the road turn R and in 15 yards (14 m) turn L down the steps and cross the footbridge. Climb back onto the cliff-top path. As you approach Bay Town you can see how the old houses huddle together beneath the cliff (5). A series of duckboards descends towards the town and

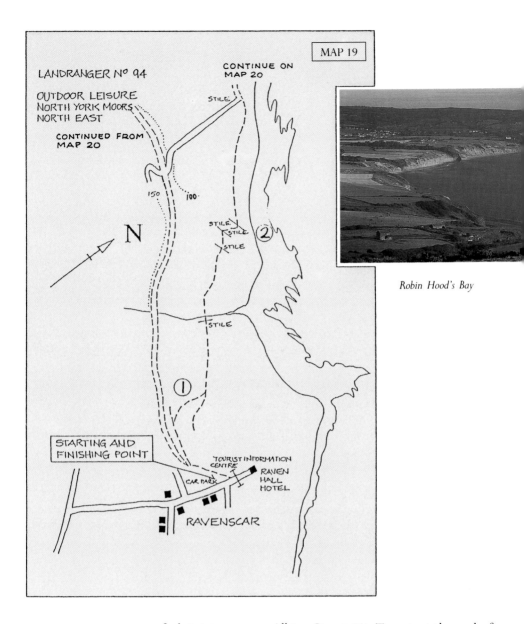

MAP 19

LANDRANGER Nº 94

OUTDOOR LEISURE
NORTH YORK MOORS
NORTH EAST

CONTINUED FROM
MAP 20

CONTINUE ON
MAP 20

STILE

150   100

N

STILE
STILE
②
STILE

STILE

STILE

①

STARTING AND
FINISHING POINT

TOURIST INFORMATION
CENTRE
CAR PARK   RAVEN
                HALL
                HOTEL

RAVENSCAR

Robin Hood's Bay

you fork L into narrow Albion Street *(6)*. Turn L at the end of
Albion Street.

The main road through Bay Town, where there is restricted
traffic access, follows the stream on your R to a bridge. It then
twists its way past the Laurel Inn *(7)* and up the steep hill to the
modern part of Robin Hood's Bay on the cliff top. Continue
past the car-parks and turn L on the road to Fylingthorpe and
Scarborough. Pass St Stephen's Church, cross the bridge and
turn L through a gate onto the old railway track.

This old railway track *(8)* is followed for some 4 miles (6.5
km). It is fringed by deciduous woodland for the first part of the
walk, which crosses lofty embankments over the valleys. There

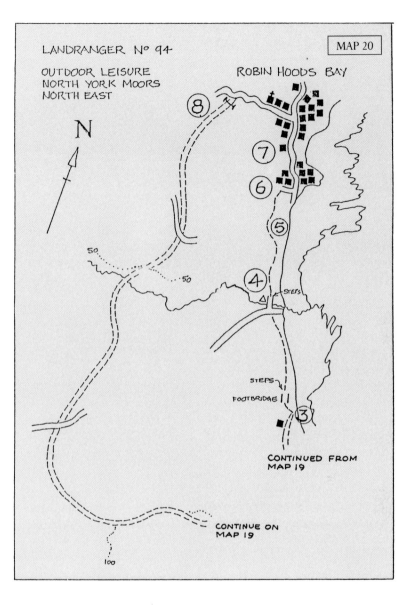

LANDRANGER Nº 94

MAP 20

OUTDOOR LEISURE
NORTH YORK MOORS
NORTH EAST

ROBIN HOODS BAY

N

50

50

STEPS

STEPS
FOOTBRIDGE

CONTINUED FROM
MAP 19

CONTINUE ON
MAP 19

100

are opportunities of seeing a variety of woodland birds. After completing a long sweep inland the track emerges above Robin Hood's Bay and offers fine sea views on the approach to Ravenscar. On the hillside to the R are a number of alum quarries. The path forks L just before the tunnel and you climb the path back to Ravenscar, turning R to the roadside carpark.

1 *The Cleveland Way* See page 53.
2 *Robin Hood's Bay*
   The older part of the village is known as Bay Town to distinguish the town from the bay. The collection of

fishermen's houses linked by narrow passages clings to the cliffside despite the pounding it receives from the sea. In 1780 the main road out of the village, King Street, was washed away and a new road had to be constructed. Part of King Street can be followed today to a point overlooking the new sea wall, built as protection in 1975.

3 *Stoupe Brow Hill*

This very steep hill once had a 1 in 2½ gradient board set at the top to warn motorists. For years it was the main highway into Robin Hood's Bay from Scarborough, horse-drawn carriages and wagons going down the hill and along the beach. The first ascent of the hill by car took place in 1912, when a Stoerwer with five passengers completed the climb. A second car only made the ascent with assistance.

4 *Boggle Hole Youth Hostel*

The building was originally Bay Town's watermill, used for grinding corn. It was destroyed by floods in 1857 and was later rebuilt.

5 *Smuggling*

Bay Town was a well-known smugglers' haunt in the late seventeenth and early eighteenth century. With the houses built so close together, it was said that a bale of silk could pass from the bottom of the village to the top without seeing daylight. This was achieved by false-backed cupboards and interlinking doors and cellars in the houses. See page 37.

6 *Inscribed stone*

Just before you reach Albion Street you pass a stone on your right inscribed 'This highway from Robin Hood's Bay over Cow Field to Farsyde Old House was finally closed by order of the Quarter Sessions, Northallerton, 1873. The existing road is by rent and sufferance'.

7 *The* Visitor *shipwreck*

The tight bend in the road at the Laurel Inn caused problems for the lifeboat being brought overland to the wreck. See page 63.

8 *The Scarborough–Whitby Railway*

The line was opened in 1885 and was one of the most scenic lines in Britain. It offered both moorland and sea views. The 21-mile-(34-km) long route had eight stations between Scarborough and Whitby West Cliff; the line reached its maximum height of 631 feet (192 m) at Ravenscar, where it entered a tunnel. A number of stations on the line offered camping coaches for holidaymakers.

Opposite *The Scars, Robin Hood's Bay*

2·17

DANBY MOORS

STARTING AND
FINISHING POINT
The Moors Centre
car-park (94-
717083). Turn
south off the A171
Guisborough to
Whitby road to
Danby, turn L for
½ mile (800 m) in
village.

LENGTH
9 miles (14 km)

ASCENT
600 feet (180 m)

This fine walk along old tracks is at its best for scenery when the heather is in bloom. The walk begins at the National Park Centre at Danby Lodge, which is well worth a visit. The route passes Siss Cross and White Cross, ancient waymarkers, and there are fine views across the moors to the coast. The return is made along the side of the Esk Valley. A compass may be required across Danby Low Moor, so the walk would be better undertaken on a fine day.

ROUTE DESCRIPTION (Maps 21, 22)

From the Moors Centre car-park *(1)* turn R up the road. At the junction take the path through the gate opposite (PFS). Follow the path through the wood to a gate and continue with a wall on your L. Turn L through the first gate and keep the wall on your L for about 50 yards (45 m), then turn half R up a track towards a stone wall, and again turn L uphill on a track to a gateway. Continue to a junction of tracks, turn L and in 20 yards (18 m) fork R. The moorland track continues around the hillside, offering views over Danby village to the dales beyond.

Cross the stream near the cottage and turn back R towards the stone cottage; continue up a stoned track which swings L to join the road. Cross the road and join an indistinct track across the moors. Set your compass for a bearing of 354° magnetic. Eventually the track peters out, but Siss Cross *(2)* on the skyline will act as a guide. The Siss Cross Road on which you are walking passes to the R of the stone and continues over the moor for a further ½ mile (800 m) to join a broad track.

Turn L and follow the track for 1½ miles (2.5 km) to White Cross *(3)*. Carry straight on at the road junction down the road to Commondale. At the bend in the road cross over to the paved way *(4)* visible on your L and turn R along the path until you see a gate on your L. Pass through the gate and cross the field, bearing half R and descending through a series of three gates to a broad track.

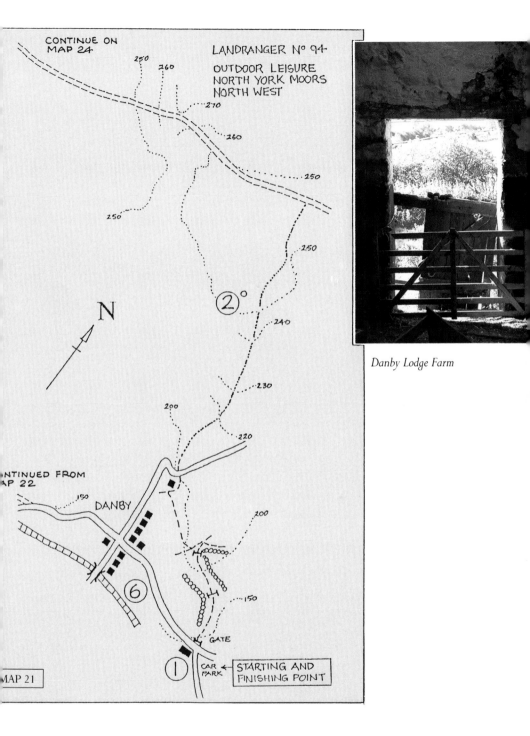

LANDRANGER N° 94

OUTDOOR LEISURE
NORTH YORK MOORS
NORTH WEST

250
260
270
260
250
250
250
250
②°
240
230
200
220

N

CONTINUED FROM
MAP 22

150
DANBY
200
⑥
150
GATE
①
CAR PARK ← STARTING AND
FINISHING POINT

MAP 21

Danby Lodge Farm

Turn L along the track, which is easy to follow and winds along the valley side with Sleddale Beck and the Esk Valley Railway *(5)* on your R. Eventually you turn R down a road and in 50 yards (45 m) turn L along Sunny Brow (PBS to Danby). The distinct track eventually passes through a silver birch wood

89

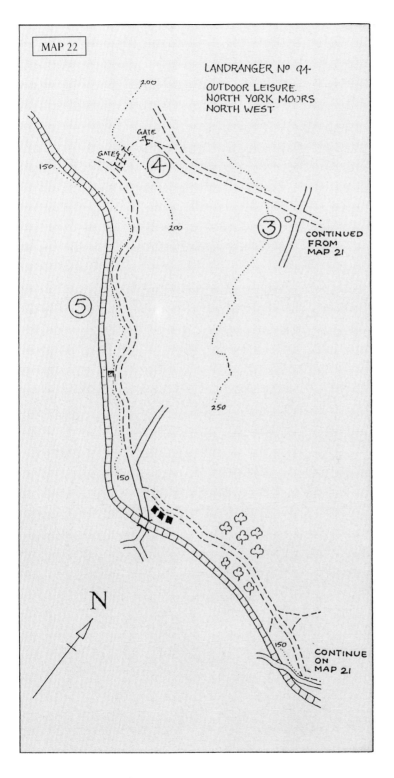

MAP 22

LANDRANGER Nº 94

OUTDOOR LEISURE.
NORTH YORK MOORS
NORTH WEST

200

GATE

GATES

④

200

150

③

CONTINUED
FROM
MAP 21

⑤

250

150

N

150

CONTINUE
ON
MAP 21

Castleton from Danby Park

91

and continues straight on to join the road. Go L along it into Danby village. Take the road opposite the junction; after a climb there are fine views on the R across the River Esk to Danby Castle (6), guarding the entrance to Little Fryup Dale. The road continues to the Moors Centre, where you turn R back to the car-park.

1 *The Moors Centre*
  The National Park Centre offers a series of displays on the history, geology, flora and fauna in the national park. There are also audio-visual displays, an information centre, cafe, picnic site and nature trail.

2 *Siss Cross*
  The rough-stone waymarker is not the original stone cross. The cross would have been set here to guide wayfarers from Danby across the moors to the Stokesley to Whitby road.

3 *White Cross* See page 68.

4 *Paved ways* See page 32.

5 *Esk Valley Railway*
  The line from Stokesley to Whitby was built over a number of years. By 1861 the line was open between Castleton and Stokesley, but it was 1865 before the line was completed to Grosmont and it was possible to run a service through to Whitby. The route is one of the most scenic on British Rail, cutting through the Leven and Esk Valleys with views of the moorland heights above. It was due for closure under the Beeching Plan but was reprieved.

6 *Danby Castle*
  The castle was built in the fourteenth century by William, Lord Latimer. It was built around a central courtyard with towers on the corners. Part of the castle is now a farmhouse and the castle is still used as the courtroom for the Court Leet, where Danby Estate matters are settled.

*Grouse butt, Danby
Low Moor*

3.18
THE BILSDALE HEAD CIRCUIT

STARTING AND FINISHING POINT
Chop Gate car-park (100-558993) at the southern end of the village on the B1257 Helmsley to Stokesley road.

LENGTH
9½ miles (15 km)

ASCENT
1750 feet (530 m)

Hasty Bank Top

The head of Bilsdale is enclosed by the highest hills on the North York Moors, rising to nearly 1500 feet (460 m). The long climb out of Bilsdale is rewarded by superb scenery and there are excellent views of the Cleveland Hills on the descent to Clay Bank. The ascent of Hasty Bank and Cold Moor offers equally impressive panoramic views over the Cleveland Plain, while the return to Chop Gate is along a ridge between Raisdale and Bilsdale. To get the most enjoyment from this walk choose a clear fine day.

ROUTE DESCRIPTION (Maps 23, 24)

From the car-park turn L through Chop Gate *(1)* village. Turn R along the road signposted to St Hilda's Church through the hamlet of Seave Green. Cross the stream and fork L up the hill,

94

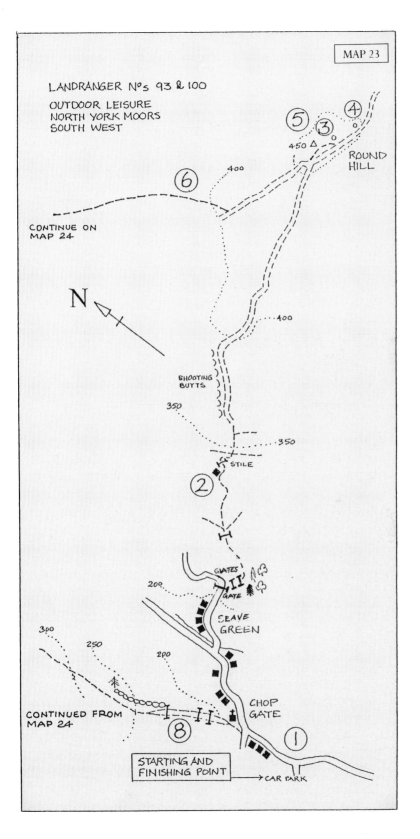

MAP 23

LANDRANGER Nºs 93 & 100

OUTDOOR LEISURE
NORTH YORK MOORS
SOUTH WEST

⑤ ③ ④

450 △

ROUND
HILL

⑥ 400

CONTINUE ON
MAP 24

N

400

SHOOTING
BUTTS

350

350

STILE

②

GATES
GATE

200

SEAVE
GREEN

300

250

200

CONTINUED FROM
MAP 24

⑧

CHOP
GATE

①

STARTING AND
FINISHING POINT

→ CAR PARK

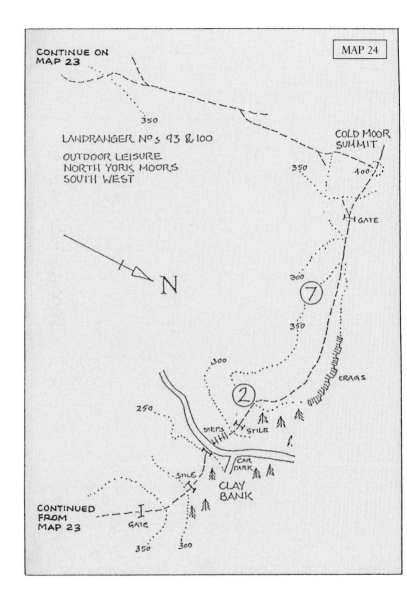

pass through a gate across the road and turn R (PBS) through two gates. The broad track swings L under the trees and begins to climb with a stone wall on your L. Pass through a gate and carry straight on up the hillside, passing a line of shale heaps *(2)*. On the skyline to the L you can see the rock outcrops of the Wainstones, which you will be passing later. Pass a stone building on your L and continue to a stile; the path then leads into a broad track across the moor.

The track follows a line of shooting butts across the moor and eventually the OS obelisk on Round Hill comes into view.

When you reach the T-junction of tracks turn R to the Hand Stone *(3)* on the L of the track. Continue along the track to the Face Stone *(4)* some 250 yards (225 m) further east, then return to the Hand Stone and turn R on the track to Round Hill *(5)*. Return to the broad track and turn R, pass the track which you came along and continue to the end of the broad path where another path bears half R across the moor *(6)*. Eventually pass through a gate and descend through a small cleft in the hillside, cross a stile and continue descending to the road at Clay Bank following a wall on your R. There may be refreshments at the car-park 100 yards (90 m) to the north.

Cross the road and climb the set of steps opposite. Cross the ladder stile and continue uphill *(2)*. A cleverly made path of stones winds its way up the hillside marked by small posts. Cross the plateau top. This is possibly the finest ridge walk in eastern England; a thousand feet below to the R is the Cleveland Plain stretching away to the River Tees and to the L the hillside tumbles away into the upper reaches of Bilsdale. At the western end of Hasty Bank are the Wainstones *(7)*, a rock outcrop offering an easy scramble into the col below. The path then climbs again, passing through a gate to the summit of Cold Moor.

On the summit turn L on the track which follows the top of the ridge. There are excellent views on your R into Raisdale and on your L into Bilsdale. After a mile take the L fork, and the path descends eventually passing above a wood and follows a stone wall to a gate. The path becomes a tree-fringed hollow way *(8)*, descending into Chop Gate. Turn L then R at the road back to the car-park.

1 *Chop Gate*
   The village name is pronounced Chop Yat, 'yat' being the local dialect word for gate.
2 *Jet mining*
   Jet has been carved around Whitby for hundreds of years. The mineral could be picked up on the sea shore after cliff falls but most of it was dug out of the hillsides around Bilsdale and the Cleveland Hills. The mineral was formed in a similar way to coal and is the fossilized remains of Monkey Puzzle trees (*Araucaria*) that have been subjected to great pressure. Some fine examples of jet jewellery can be seen in Whitby Museum. See page 75.
3 *The Hand Stone*
   The stone is so-called because of the hand carved on it to

97

indicate the direction to travel. It probably marked the directions over the moor to Kirkbymoorside to the south and Stokesley to the north.

4 *The Face Stone*

The ancient stone incorporates the carved figure of a face. Set at the junction of a number of moorland tracks, it stands on the old Cleveland boundary.

5 *Round Hill, Botton Head*

This is the highest point of the North York Moors, at 1489 feet (454 m) above sea level, though the views are not good from the actual summit. In October 1940 an Armstrong Whitley bomber failed to climb over the hill and crashed into the north face. Pieces of wreckage still remain on the hillside.

6 *Ingleby Botton*

There are views to the R as you walk along the path into the valley of Ingleby Botton. You can look back to the steep north face of Botton Head and across the valley to the slanted track which climbs the opposite hillside. This was the incline on the Rosedale Railway where ironstone wagons were hauled on and off the moors. See page 28.

7 *The Wainstones* See page 75.

8 *Hollow way*

These ancient tracks from the moors have been used for centuries to bring peat and goods into the village. The frequent use of these tracks has created a deep hollow below the level of the surrounding fields.

The Wainstones

3·19

THE HERITAGE COAST PATH

STARTING AND
FINISHING POINT
Ravenscar car-park
(94-980014).
Turn east off the
A171 Scarborough
to Whitby road.

LENGTH
12 miles (19 km)

ASCENT
1000 feet (300 m)

South of Ravenscar stretch miles of peaceful coastline. The cliffs tumble away, sometimes to the sea or to the Undercliff, offering splendid views. There are two descents with easy access to the shore at Hayburn Wyke and Cloughton Wyke. The return is made along the disused railway track. The route-finding is simple throughout the walk.

ROUTE DESCRIPTION (Maps 25, 26)

From the car-park turn L, walk down the road and turn R along Station Road *(1)*. After 50 yards (45 m) turn L at the end of the wire fence and follow the path down to the cliff top, then turn R. The savage coastline below was the scene of the shipwreck of the *Coronation* in 1913 and the *Fred Everard* in 1965 *(2)*. The path continues south along the cliff top for 3½ miles (5.5 km). Pass a coastguard station and continue with the Undercliff *(3)* below.

As you approach Hayburn Wyke on a clear day you can see Scarborough Castle and Filey Brigg in the distance *(4)*. Eventually the path passes over a stile and descends into Hayburn Wyke Woods *(5)* down a series of steps. Ignore the stile signposted to Staintondale and bear half L. The second footbridge in the wood crosses Hayburn Wyke Beck, and then a path to the L leads to the beach where there is a small waterfall.

Continue straight along the path which begins to climb up the hillside. Fork L at the two junctions and you will arrive back at the cliff-top path. After 1¼ miles (2 km) the path descends into Cloughton Wyke. At the bottom turn R up some steps and pass a small car-park. The track becomes a surfaced road. Cross a bridge and turn R over a stile, then descend to the former railway track and turn L. This was the route of the Whitby–Scarborough railway line *(6)*.

The track is followed all the way to Ravenscar passing on the way the sites of Hayburn Wyke and Staintondale stations. The climbing is hardly noticeable, but between Staintondale and Ravenscar the ascent is a 1 in 41 gradient. When you reach

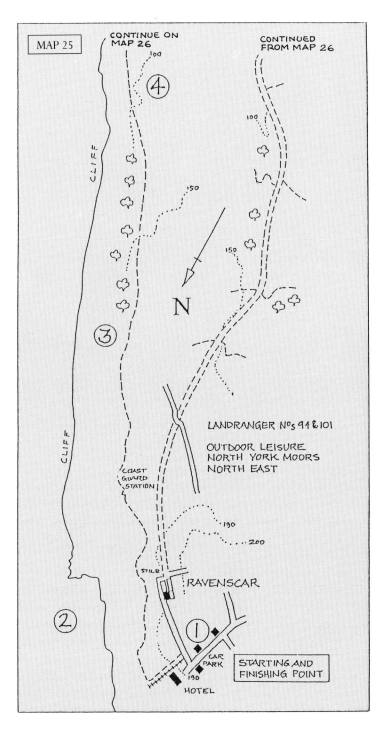

MAP 25

Ravenscar, pass over a stile beside the gate and take the track to the R of the platform; cross Station Square and turn L down Station Road, turning L again to the car-park.

Cliff top path near
Hayburn Wyke

1 *Ravenscar*

The Raven Hall Hotel stands on the site of a Roman signal station. There were plans in the 1890s to develop the village into a major seaside resort but, the scheme collapsed. The 600 feet (180 m) high cliffs which separated the proposed new town from the sea would have been a problem.

2 *The* Coronation *and* Fred Everard *shipwrecks*

The 3290 ton (3237 tonne) *Coronation* ran aground on 11 January 1913 in a snow storm. The distress signals went unnoticed in the storm, but the crew rowed a boat ashore and rigged a line and bosun's chair to take everyone off the ship. Various attempts were made to refloat the ship all through the spring and summer, but it was September before she was refloated and taken to Hartlepool. After all the effort the ship was burned out at Hartlepool a month later.

The 1542 ton (1567 tonne) motor vessel *Fred Everard* ran ashore at nearly the same place in a snow storm on 27 November 1965. The crew were saved by Whitby lifeboat. This ship broke up within weeks and parts of the wreck may be visible at low tide.

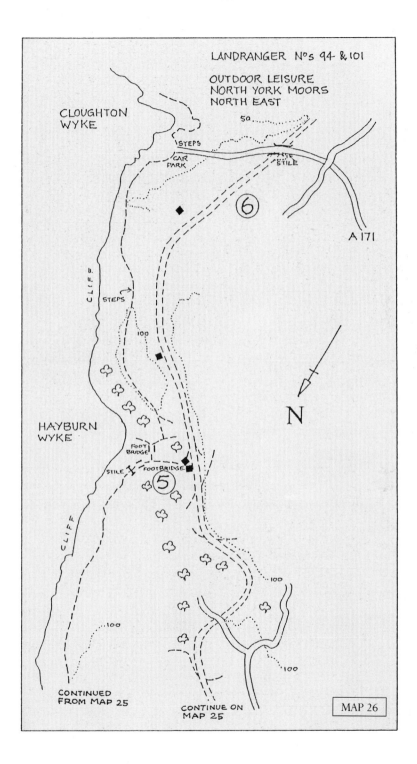

LANDRANGER Nºs 94 & 101

OUTDOOR LEISURE
NORTH YORK MOORS
NORTH EAST

CLOUGHTON
WYKE

50

STEPS

CAR
PARK

STILE
STILE

⑥

A 171

CLIFF

STEPS

100

HAYBURN
WYKE

FOOT
BRIDGE

STILE   FOOTBRIDGE

⑤

CLIFF

100

100

100

CONTINUED
FROM MAP 25

CONTINUE ON
MAP 25

MAP 26

103

3 *The Undercliff or Beast Cliff*
This long shelf-like plateau lies some 200 feet (60 m) down the cliff face. The undisturbed woodland and scrub now forms an interesting area for naturalists. It has been designated as a Site of Special Scientific Interest and may become a nature reserve.

4 *The Cleveland Way*
Filey Brigg is the end of the Cleveland Way and this is the walker's first sight of his goal. See page 53.

5 *Hayburn Wyke Nature Reserve*
The nature reserve was created around the wooded banks of Hayburn Beck. The wood consists mainly of oak, with ash, hazel and hawthorn. Among the plants to be seen in early summer are woodruff, enchanter's nightshade, lady's mantle, common spotted orchid and wild honeysuckle. The chiff-chaff can be heard and there are treecreepers, blackcaps and redstarts.

6 *Whitby–Scarborough Railway* See page 87.

The waterfall, Hayburn Wyke

105

3·20

THE FARNDALE HEAD CIRCUIT

STARTING AND
FINISHING POINT
Low Mill car-park,
Farndale (94-
673952). From
Kirkbymoorside
take the road to
Gillamoor and
continue on the
Hutton-le-Hole
road, turning L to
Low Mill.

LENGTH
16 miles (26 km)

ASCENT
1000 feet (300 m)

This long walk is easy to follow once you have climbed out of Farndale and until you descend again into the valley. This leaves you free to enjoy the fine views from the ancient ridgeway and along the bed of the disused mineral railway.

ROUTE DESCRIPTION (Maps 27–30)

From the car-park turn R up the narrow road. After 400 yards (375 m) turn L over a cattle grid (PBS to Rudland Rigg). Walk up the track to Horn End Farm, at the junction of tracks walk straight on and pass through a gate. The track crosses the field to another gate then begins to swing R through more gates, eventually passing a stone barn on your L. Walk between the stone walls, pass through a gate, ignore the next gate and bear half L (PBS) on a track which leads to a footbridge.

After crossing the stream, walk up the field to a stile beside a gate. Follow the track which bears L but soon swings round to the R and climbs through the bracken onto Rudland Rigg (1). Bear R along the ridge road; after 1½ miles (2.5 km) you pass the remains of Cockan Cross (2) and just over ½ mile (800 m) later the Cammon Stone (3). Continue on the broad track to Bloworth Crossing (4) 1¼ miles (2 km) further on, where you reach a junction. At this remote point high on the moors turn R along the disused railway line. This is an easy way to traverse the moors as the mineral railway went into cuttings through the high ground and the streams are crossed on high embankments.

The rugged heights of Upper Farndale gradually descend into the head of the valley as you continue down the track, which has become popular with walkers (5). After 3 miles (5 km) you pass a track to the L which descends to Esklets, a ruined farm near the source of the River Esk. You continue on the railway with Farndale (6) on the R for 2¾ miles (4.5 km) to Blakey Bank. As you approach Blakey Bank you pass close to the Lion Inn, which may be of interest during opening hours.

Approaching Blakey Bank the former railway passed through

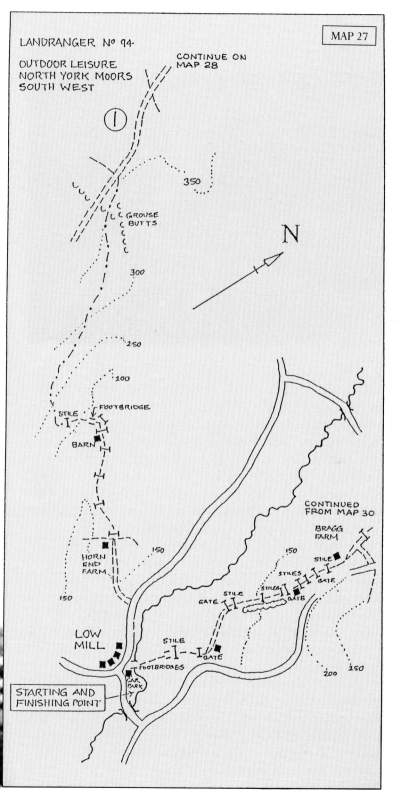

LANDRANGER Nº 94

OUTDOOR LEISURE
NORTH YORK MOORS
SOUTH WEST

CONTINUE ON
MAP 28

MAP 27

①

350

GROUSE
BUTTS

N

300

250

100

STILE   FOOTBRIDGE

BARN

CONTINUED
FROM MAP 30

BRAGG
FARM

STILE

150

STILES

HORN
END
FARM

150

STILE

GATE   STILE

150

STILE

GATE

LOW
MILL

STILE

GATE

FOOTBRIDGES

CAR
PARK

STARTING AND
FINISHING POINT

200   250

107

The Rudland Rigg Road

a tunnel under the road, but this is now blocked. Bear half R to the road, turn L to the junction and pick up the track opposite (PFS to Rosedale) then turn R on the railway going south *(7)*. Pass a 'Private no road' sign and continue down the track for a mile (1.6 km). To the L is an excellent view over Rosedale to East Mines. After a mile (1.6 km) turn R at a small cairn and pass the ruins of Sledge Shoe House which are just visible from the railway track. An indistinct track leads across the heather moorland ridge to join the road near a line of shooting butts.

The indistinct path continues through the heather just to the north of the butts. A good view of Farndale opens up as you begin to descend into the dale. Head for a gate in a stone wall where a hollow way *(8)* leads down to the bottom of a field. Turn L, keeping the stone wall on your R and pass through a series of gates which lead to the road. Cross the road, take the lane opposite past the stone cottage and turn L at the PFS just before Bragg Farm.

The next section is well waymarked. Bear half R (PFS) across the field to a stone stile and continue above Bitchagreen Farm. Pass through a gate and cross the field to a stile and then continue to a ladder stile. Bear half R over a field to a gate and continue on a paved way with a hedge on your L. Turn R at the stile and gate and cross the field into a farm lane. Turn R through a gate in the farmyard, this leads to a stile and bridge

108

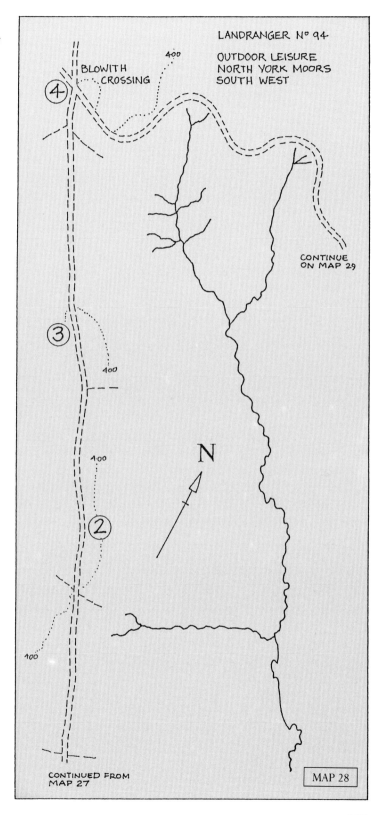

LANDRANGER Nº 94

OUTDOOR LEISURE
NORTH YORK MOORS
SOUTH WEST

BLOWITH
CROSSING

400

④

CONTINUE
ON MAP 29

③

400

400

N

②

400

CONTINUED FROM
MAP 27

MAP 28

109

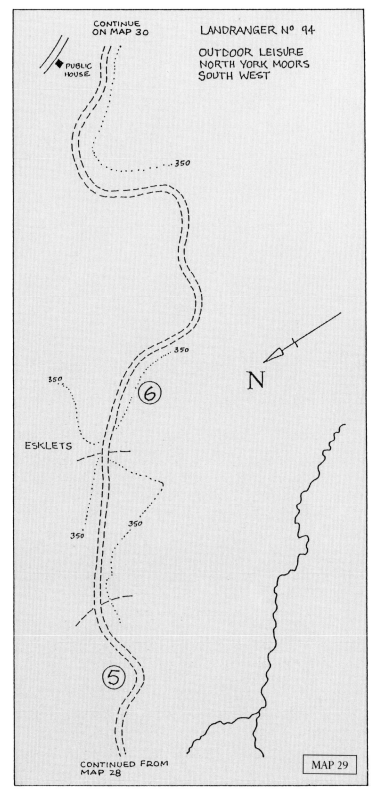

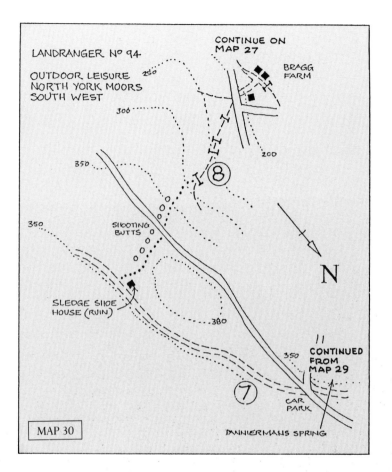

over a stream. A paved way crosses the field to a footbridge which leads back to the car-park in Low Mill.

1 Rudland Rigg
This ancient ridge route over the moors has probably been in use for 2,000 years. It would offer a reasonably dry north–south route over the rugged moors.

2 Cockan Cross
The broken shaft stands in a socket stone. The stone is inscribed 'Farndale; Stoxle Rode (Stokesley Road); Bransdale; Kirby Rode (Kirkbymoorside Road)'.

3 Cammon Stone
This large upright slab may have been erected as a waymarker in prehistoric times. There is a Hebrew inscription on the west side of the stone, placed there in more recent times.

4 Bloworth Crossing
This was the site of a level crossing on the Rosedale Ironstone

111

Railway, which gives some indication of the amount of traffic on the road last century. It would be a hardy life for the crossing keeper and his family, 1200 feet (365 m) above sea level on these exposed moors.

5 *Long distance walks*

This ideal walking track is also used by walkers on the 40 mile (64 km) Lyke Wake Walk and the 190 mile (306 km) Coast to Coast Walk.

6 *Upper Farndale*

There have been plans put forward at various times since the 1930s to flood this part of the valley and create a reservoir, possibly turning the track into a road to bring in construction material. Fortunately the plans have so far been successfully resisted.

7 *Rosedale Ironstone Railway*

At this point the mineral railway split into two spurs, one heading north around the head of Rosedale to the East Mines which can be seen at the other side of the valley. Our route turned south to Sheriff's Pit and Rosedale Chimney (see page 26).

8 *Hollow Way* See page 99.

Farndale from Pannierman's Spring

3·21

HELMSLEY CIRCUIT

STARTING AND
FINISHING POINT
Helmsley Market
Place (100-
612837).

LENGTH
18 miles (29 km)

ASCENT
1675 feet (510 m)

This is a delightful day's walking using a combination of field, moorland and woodland paths to visit Rievaulx Abbey and the Upper Rye Valley. There are fine views from Rievaulx and Helmsley Moors before returning down wooded Beckdale. This is a quiet walk away from the crowds.

ROUTE DESCRIPTION (Maps 31–34)

From the Market Place take the road past the church entrance, cross over the road and walk down Cleveland Way (PFS to Rievaulx). The lane rises steadily, offering views of Helmsley Castle (1). Eventually turn L over a stile (PFS) and follow the edge of the field with a fence on your L. At the end turn R alongside the wood. Cross two stiles and fork L through a gate into the wood. The path descends, crosses a track in the valley bottom and climbs back out of the valley. This leads to two gates and the route then crosses a field to a stile in front of Griff Lodge. There is an excellent view on the L down to the River Rye.

Pass over the stile and continue on the track with a wood on your L. Eventually cross a stile and descend through Quarry Bank Wood to the road. Turn L and just before Rievaulx Bridge (2) turn R on the road to Rievaulx Abbey (3) which is now in sight. Pass the entrance to Rievaulx Abbey on your R, unless you wish to visit the site, continue round the sweeping bend and then turn L through a gate (PFS to Bow Bridge).

As you cross the stream you can see Rievaulx Mill (4) on your R. Pass through a gate into a hedged lane, continue with a wire fence and former canal (5) on your R. Cross the stiles near the river, walk across the field, then over a stile which gives access to a lane. Turn L over Bow Bridge (2) then turn R (PFS to Hawnby) to continue to the L of the river. After a while cross a stile into a wood beside the River Rye, then cross a field to join a farm road and turn R. There are pleasant views of the wooded hillside and tree-fringed river.

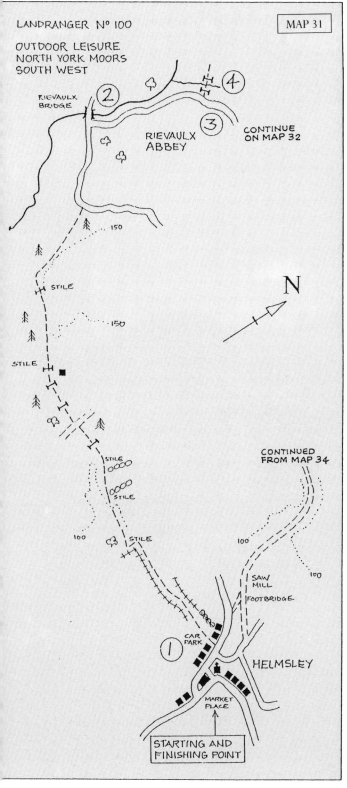

OUTDOOR LEISURE
NORTH YORK MOORS
SOUTH WEST

RIEVAULX
BRIDGE

② ④

③

RIEVAULX
ABBEY

CONTINUE
ON MAP 32

150

STILE

150

STILE

N

STILE

STILE

CONTINUED
FROM MAP 34

STILE

100

100

100

SAW
MILL

FOOTBRIDGE

CAR
PARK

①

HELMSLEY

MARKET
PLACE

STARTING AND
FINISHING POINT

*Sunlight in the West
Range of Helmsley
Castle*

Overleaf *Helmsley
Castle*

At the junction turn R to Tylas Farm. Turn L in the farmyard along a farm road to Barnclose Farm. Turn L in this farmyard to a gate, then turn R to a gate and stile. Continue with a hedge on your R, after 100 yards (90 m) bear half L up the field to a stile then turn R along the edge of the wood. There is a view ahead to Hawnby Hill with Easterside to the R. Continue along the hillside and join a farm road near a cattle grid. Turn R along the road to Shaken Bridge Farm, curve R through the yard, then turn L down to the road keeping a fence on your L.

Turn R over the bridge then turn L (PBS) on a track through a wood, which may have daffodils or rhododendrons in flower, depending on the season. At the gate turn L up the farm road. Turn back half R just before the thatched farmhouse at Broadway Foot, where there is a fine prospect across Upper Ryedale. Follow the wire fence on your R; the path swings L to a gate and continues to join a forest road; bear L to a junction then turn back R on a forest road which rises to a gate and the main road.

Turn L on the grass beside the road to the top of the hill. You are going to turn R on a track (PFS to Cow House Bank), but there is a magnificent view down Bilsdale from the top of the hill and a stone observation point which is well worth a visit.

Walk along the broad track towards Cow House Bank; as you leave the trees you cross the edge of Rievaulx Moor and views over the moors open up to the north. After 2½ miles (4 km) you reach a minor road from Helmsley. Continue on the track on the opposite side, passing two metal sculptures (6) for a further 1¼ miles (3 km) to Cow House Bank, where there are further extensive views over Bonfield Gill to Birk Nab (7).

Turn R down the road for ¾ mile (1.2 km) then turn R along a farm road to Carlton Grange Farm. Walk straight past the farm and turn L over a stile along the side of the field, then turn R at the end of the field into the wood. The track bears slightly R into a small valley, then, out of the other side of the wood, cross a field with a hedge on your L to a road. Turn L past High Baxton's Farm then turn R into a field (PFS). Turn R at the end of the field, then L through a gate and cross another field into the wood. Turn L and follow the path just inside the edge of the wood.

Eventually the path leads into a small side valley. Take the path on the far side of this valley which descends steeply and swings L into the main valley. Cross the stream and follow the path, which gradually climbs up the opposite side, then forks L towards the valley bottom, continuing along the valley side until

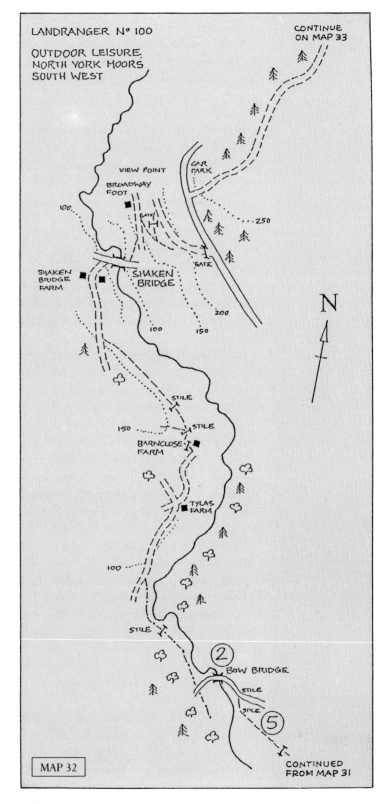

OUTDOOR LEISURE.
NORTH YORK MOORS
SOUTH WEST

VIEW POINT

BROADWAY
FOOT

CAR
PARK

100

250

GATE

SHAKEN
BRIDGE
FARM

SHAKEN
BRIDGE

GATE

N

100

200

150

150

STILE

STILE

150

BARNCLOSE
FARM

TYLAS
FARM

100

STILE

2

BOW BRIDGE

STILE

STILE

5

MAP 32

CONTINUED
FROM MAP 31

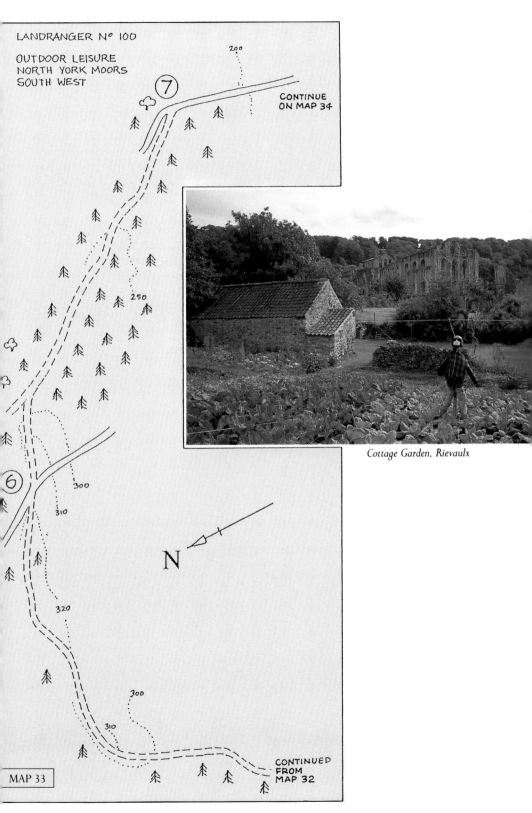

LANDRANGER Nº 100

OUTDOOR LEISURE
NORTH YORK MOORS
SOUTH WEST

⑦

200

CONTINUE
ON MAP 34

250

⑥

300

310

320

300

310

Cottage Garden, Rievaulx

N

MAP 33

CONTINUED
FROM
MAP 32

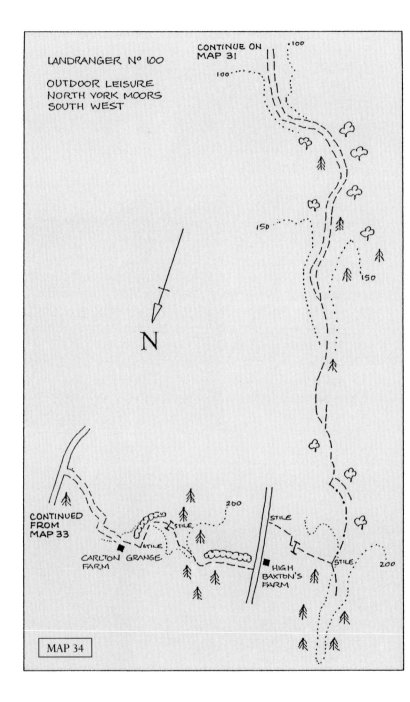

you fork L to join a stoned track. This track winds its way between the steep-sided, wooded slopes, eventually passing a saw mill. Continue on the road until it starts to climb, then fork R on a track which follows the stream, cross a footbridge and continue to the road into Helmsley. Carry straight on to the church and Market Place.

1 *Helmsley Castle*

The castle was built about 1200. It was besieged by Parliamentary forces after the Battle of Marston Moor. Colonel Crosland, who defended the castle, finally negotiated honourable terms for the surrender of the castle, after an attempt to raise the seige failed. He surrendered the castle on 22 November 1644 and two years later it was made unfit for war.

2 *Rievaulx Bridge and Bow Bridge*

During a severe flood in Ryedale in 1754, Rievaulx Bridge and Shaken Bridge were destroyed. The original wooden Bow Bridge was also swept away by the flood.

3 *Rievaulx Abbey*

Extensive ruins remain to give some idea of this large and powerful abbey. It was the first Cistercian abbey in Yorkshire and was founded in 1131 by Walter L'Espec. At the height of its power during the time of Abbot Aelred (1147–1166) the abbey had 140 choir monks and 600 lay brothers.

4 *Rievaulx Mill*

The water-powered mill was used for grinding corn and was in use until 1960.

5 *Rievaulx Canal*

The canal was cut to allow the easier transport of stone for the building of Rievaulx Abbey. The River Rye was diverted along the canal and stone was floated on rafts to the abbey.

6 *Aluminium sculptures*

Two large, irregular-shaped rings standing some 8 feet (2.4 m) high — the work of sculptor Austin Wright — were erected by the Yorkshire Arts Association in 1977. One of the rings has since been vandalized and removed. The surrounding moors are often home to rare birds of prey and it is worth scanning the skies from this viewpoint.

7 *Birk Nab and the Missing Link*

Birk Nab is the 1000 feet (300 m) summit of a long ridge descending towards Helmsley. This is the last climb for walkers on the 50 mile (80 km) Missing Link. The route was pioneered in 1975 by June and Pete Gough, Colin Hood, and

Maurice and Malcolm Boyes. The Cleveland Way forms a 112 mile (180 km) horseshoe around the western, northern and eastern sides of the North York Moors, the Missing Link heads back across the forest, moors and valleys on the southern side of the North York Moors, linking fourteen fine view-points. Walkers undertaking the full route can start or finish anywhere, making access easier. The Missing Link can also be walked as a separate route.

From Crook Ness on the coast near Burniston the route heads west through Langdale Forest, crosses the River Derwent and follows the edge of Crosscliff to Saltergate. The route crosses moorland to Levisham then passes through Cropton Forest and over the moors to the delightful villages of Lastingham and Hutton-le-Hole. Farndale and Sleightholme Dale are traversed before Birk Nab is climbed and the walker heads south down Riccaldale to Helmsley. There is no time limit to the 50-mile (80-km) walk and usually it is undertaken in two or three days.

Rievaulx Abbey Church

APPENDICES

ACCESS FOR THE WALKER

It is important to realize at the outset that the designation of a National Park does not change the ownership of land within it in any way. In the case of the North York Moors National Park, for example, only 2% of the land area is owned by the Park Authority, compared to the 76.5% of the land which is privately owned. The laws of access and trespass apply just as much to areas of private land within a National Park as to those outside the boundaries.

The National Parks and Access to the Countryside Act of 1949 required County Councils in England and Wales to prepare maps which showed all paths over which the public had a right to walk. The final form of the map is referred to as a definitive map and copies are held at the offices of the County Council and District Council and sometimes by the Community Council concerned. Paths can only be diverted or deleted from a definitive map by the raising of a Division Order or an Extinguishment Order respectively. The paths are classified as either footpaths (for walkers only) or bridleways (for walkers, horseriders and cyclists). These public rights-of-way were included on the now withdrawn one inch to one mile (1:63 360) Seventh Series, the 1:25 000 Second Series (i.e. Pathfinder), 1:50 000 First and Second Series (i.e. Landranger) and the Outdoor Leisure maps.

NATIONAL TRUST AREAS
Currently the National Trust owns 1% of the area of the National Trust. The Trust's policy is to give free access at all times to its open spaces. However, there cannot be unrestricted access to tenanted farms, young plantations and woods, or certain nature reserves where the preservation of rare flora and fauna is paramount.

FORESTRY COMMISSION FOREST
The Commission allows the public access wherever possible throughout its forest, but it should be emphasized that some of the routes described in this book use permissive paths and not rights-of-way. Forestry operations occur throughout the forests and walkers should keep clear of any working sites and obey any working notices. Always behave in a sensible manner and cause no damage.

PERMITTED OR PERMISSIVE PATHS
The former Rosedale mineral railway used in Walks 4 and 20 between Bank Top and Blakey Junction is not a right-of-way, but Spaunton Estate allows walkers to use the track. The bed of the former Scarborough–Whitby railway used in Walks 16 and 19 is now owned by Scarborough Borough Council and is a permitted path for walkers.

SAFETY

The routes described in this guide vary considerably in both length and difficulty. Some of the easy walks should, with reasonable care, be safe at any time of the year and in almost any weather conditions; the more difficult walks on the other hand, using the high moorland cross-country routes, can be arduous in bad weather. These should be undertaken in winter only by groups of well-equipped and experienced walkers.

It cannot be emphasized too strongly that weather conditions can change very rapidly. What is a drizzle in a valley could be a blizzard on the moor top. Select clothing and equipment for the worst weather you may encounter. Two compentent rescue teams are available by police call-out. If you meet with an accident, either to one of your own party or by discovering someone else injured, give what First Aid you are capable of administering. If necessary, shelter the casualty. Write down the grid reference of the incident, and then locate the nearest village or telephone. Ideally two people should go for assistance, leaving someone behind with the casualty, but obviously the decision will be determined by the number in the party.

The golden rules for safety in mountain and moorland areas are:

DO

Carry appropriate clothing and equipment, all of which should be in sound condition.

Carry the correct map and a compass and be practised in their use.

Leave a note of your intended route (and keep to it!).

Report your return as soon as possible.

Keep warm, but not overwarm, at all times.

Eat nourishing foods and rest at regular intervals.

Avoid becoming exhausted.

Know First Aid and the correct procedure in case of accidents or illness.

Obtain a weather forecast before you start. Check the local telephone directory under Weathercall.

Keep together if walking in a group; place a strong walker at the back to assist stragglers.

DO NOT

Go out on your own unless you are experienced; four is a good number for a party.

Leave any member of a party behind.

Climb sea cliffs or crags without experience.

Attempt routes which are beyond your skill and experience.

Walk on the cliff-top paths at night; allow plenty of time to clear the cliffs.

A booklet titled *Moorland Safety* is available from the North York Moors National Park Information Service.

The North York Moors are the home of the adder, Britain's only poisonous snake. They are shy creatures and will only attack if threatened or startled. If someone is bitten reassure the casualty that it is unusual for anyone to die from an adder bite but that it can be painful. Clean away any venom from around the wound; stop the casualty walking and then send for assistance.

GIVING A GRID REFERENCE

Giving a grid reference is an excellent way of 'pin-pointing' a feature, such as a church or mountain summit, on an Ordnance Survey map.

Grid lines, which are used for this purpose, are shown on the 1:25 000 Outdoor Leisure, 1:25 000 Pathfinder and 1:50 000 Landranger maps produced by the Ordnance Survey; these are the maps most commonly used by walkers. They are the thin blue lines (one kilometre apart) going vertically and horizontally across the map producing a network of small squares. Each line, whether vertical or horizontal, is given a number from 00 to 99, with the sequence repeating itself every 100 lines. The 00 lines are slightly thicker than the others thus producing large squares with sides made up of 100 small squares and thus representing 100 kilometres. Each of these large squares is identified by two letters. The entire network of lines covering the British Isles, excluding Ireland, is called the National Grid.

FIGURE 3 Giving a grid reference

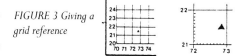

This shows a corner of an Ordnance Survey 1:50 000 Landranger map which contains a Youth Hostel. Using this map, the method of determining a grid reference is as follows:

Step 1

Holding the map in the normal upright position, note the number of the 'vertical' grid line to the left of the hostel. This is 72.

Step 2

Now imagine that the space between this grid line and the adjacent one to the right of the hostel is divided into ten equal divisions (the diagram on the right does this for you). Estimate the number of these 'tenths' that the hostel lies to the right of the left-hand grid line. This is 8. Add this to the number found in Step 1 to make 728.

Step 3

Note the number of the grid line below the hostel and add it on to the number obtained above. This is 21, so that the number becomes 72821.

Step 4

Repeat Step 2 for the space containing the hostel, but now in a vertical direction. The final number to be added is 5, making 728215. This is called a six-figure grid reference. This, coupled with the number or name of the appropriate Landranger or Outdoor Leisure map, will enable the Youth Hostel to be found.

A full grid reference will also include the identification of the appropriate 100 kilometre square of the National Grid; for example, SD 728215. This information is given in the margin of each map.

COUNTRYSIDE ACCESS CHARTER

YOUR RIGHTS OF WAY ARE:
- public footpaths — on foot only;
- bridleways — on foot, horseback and pedal cycle;
- byways (usually old roads), most 'roads used as public paths' and, of course, public roads — all traffic.

Use maps and signs — Ordnance Survey Pathfinder and Landranger maps show most public rights of way — or look for paths that have coloured waymarking arrows — yellow on footpaths, blue on bridleways, red on tracks that can be legally used by vehicles.

ON RIGHTS OF WAY YOU CAN:
- take a pram, pushchair or wheelchair if practicable;
- take a dog (on a lead or under close control);
- take a short route round an illegal obstruction or remove it sufficiently to get past.

YOU HAVE A RIGHT TO GO FOR RECREATION TO:
- public parks and open spaces — on foot;
- most commons near older towns and cities — on foot and sometimes on horseback;
- private land where the owner has a formal agreement with the local authority.

IN ADDITION:
You can use the following by local or established custom or consent — ask for advice if you're unsure:
- many areas of open country like mountain, moorland, fell and coastal areas, especially those of the National Trust, and most commons;
- some woods and forest, especially those owned by the Forestry Commission;
- country parks and picnic sites;
- most beaches;
- towpaths on canals and rivers;
- some land that is being rested from agriculture, where notices allowing access are displayed;
- some private paths and tracks.

Consent sometimes extends to riding horses and pedal cycles.

FOR YOUR INFORMATION:
- county and metropolitan district councils and London boroughs have a duty to protect, maintain and record rights of way, and hold registers of commons and village greens — report problems you find to them;
- obstructions, dangerous animals, harassment and misleading signs on rights of way are illegal;
- if a public path runs along the edge of a field it must not be ploughed or disturbed;
- a public path across a field can be ploughed or disturbed to cultivate a crop, but the surface must be quickly restored and the line of the path made apparent on the ground;
- crops (other than grass) must not be allowed to inconvenience the use of a right of way, or prevent the line from being apparent on the ground;
- landowners can require you to leave land to which you have no right of access;
- motor vehicles are normally permitted only on roads, byways and some 'roads used as public paths';
- follow any local bylaws.

AND, WHERE YOU GO, FOLLOW THE COUNTRY CODE:
- enjoy the countryside and respect its life and work;
- guard against all risk of fire;
- fasten all gates;
- keep your dogs under close control;
- keep to public paths across farmland;
- use gates and stiles to cross fences, hedges and walls;
- leave livestock, crops and machinery alone;
- take your litter home;
- help to keep all water clean;
- protect wildlife, plants and trees;
- take special care on country roads;
- make no unnecessary noise.

Addresses of Useful Organizations

British Trust for Conservation Volunteers
36 St Mary's Street, Wallingford, Oxfordshire,
OX10 0EU
Tel: (01491) 824 602

The Camping and Caravanning Club
Greenfields House, Westwood Way, Coventry,
CV4 8JH
Tel: (01203) 694 995

Council for National Parks
246 Lavender Hill, London, SW11 1LJ
Tel: (0171) 924 4077

Countryside Commission
John Dower House, Crescent Place, Cheltenham,
Gloucestershire, GL50 3RA
Tel: (01242) 521 381

English Nature
North Minster Road, Peterborough, PE1 1UA
Tel: (01733) 340 345

The Long Distance Walkers Association
10 Temple Park Close, Leeds, LS15 0JJ
Tel: (01132) 642 205

National Trust
Yorkshire Regional Office, The Goddards,
27 Tadcaster Road, Dringhouses, York,
YO2 2QG
Tel: (01904) 702 021

North York Moors Association
7 The Avenue, Nunthorpe, Middlesbrough
Tel: (01642) 316 412

North York Moors Forest District
42 Eastgate, Pickering, North Yorkshire
Tel: (01751) 473 810

North York Moors Historical Railway Trust
Pickering Station, Pickering, North Yorkshire
Tel: (01751) 472 508

North York Moors National Park Information
Service
The Old Vicarage, Bondgate, Helmsley, York,
YO6 5BP
Tel: (01642) 316 412

North Yorkshire County Council
County Hall, Northallerton
Tel: (01609) 780 780

Ramblers' Association
1/5 Wandsworth Road
London, SW8 2XX
Tel: (0171) 582 6878

Ryedale Folk Museum
Hutton-le-Hole, York, YO6 6UA
Tel: (01751) 417 367

Yorkshire and Humberside Regional Office
Countryside Commission, Victoria Wharf
Embankment IV, Sovereign Street, Leeds,
LS1 4BA
Tel: (01132) 469 222

Yorkshire and Humberside Tourist Board
312 Tadcaster Road, York, YO2 2HF
Tel: (01904) 707 961

Yorkshire Water Services
2 The Embankment, Sovereign Street, Leeds,
LS1 4BG
Tel: (01132) 343 234

Yorkshire Wildlife Trust and Yorkshire
Naturalists' Trust
10 Toft Green, York, YO1 1JT
Tel: (01904) 659 570

Youth Hostels Association (England and Wales)
Trevelyan House, 8 St Stephen's Hill, St Albans,
Hertfordshire, AL1 2DY
Tel: (01727) 855 215

Tourist Information Centres
Danby *Tel*: (01287) 660 654
Great Ayton *Tel*: (01642) 722 835
Guisborough *Tel*: (01287) 633 801
Helmsley *Tel*: (01439) 770 173
Malton *Tel*: (01653) 600 048
Pickering *Tel*: (01751) 473 791
Scarborough *Tel*: (01723) 373 333
Sutton Bank *Tel*: (01845) 597 426
Thirsk *Tel* (01545) 522 755
Whitby *Tel*: (01947) 602 674

INDEX

Place names and sites of interest only are included. Page numbers in *italics* refer to illustrations.

Airy Holme Farm 79, 82

Bay Town, *see* Robin Hood's Bay
Beck Hole 39, 44
Beggar's Bridge, Esk Valley 30, 32
Bilsdale 6, 94–99, 117
Birk Nab 117, 121
Blakey Bank 106
Blakey Topping 49
Bloworth Crossing 106, 111
Botton Head 97, 99
Bridestones 19–21, *21*

Cammon Stone 106, 111
Captain Cook Cottage, Staithes 37
Captain Cook Monument 77, 82
Captain Cook Museum 77, 80, 82
Castleton *90*
Chop Gate 94, 97
Cleveland Hills 6, 73–76
Cloughton Wyke 100
Cockan Cross 106, 111
Cold Moor 73, 97
Commondale 64–68
Cringle Moor *73*, 75

Dalby Forest Drive 29
Danby Castle 93
Danby Moors 88–93
Derwent, River 123
Donna Cross 75
Dove, River 6, 22, *24*
Dundale, Pond 45, 49, 72

Easby Moor 77
Egton Bridge 30, 31, 32, *33*
Esk, River 30–33, 58, 106
Esk Valley 30–33, 88, 93
Esk Valley (hamlet) 39, 44
Esk Valley Railway 15, 42, 89, 93
Esk Valley Way 32

Face Stone 99
Farndale 6, 22–25, 106–113, 123

Farwath 69, 72
Fylingdales, RAF 49

Garbutt Wood 17
Glaisdale 30, 32
Goathland 42
Gormire, Lake 17
Great Ayton 77, *80*
Grosmont 15, 39, 44, 54

Hackness 6, 54, 57
Hambleton Drove Road 50, 53
Hand Stone 99
Hasty Bank 6, 73, *94*, 97
Hayburn Wyke 6, 100, *102*, *104*,
    105
Helmsley 114, 121
Helmsley Castle 114, *116*, 121
Hilda Wood 6, *56*, 57
Hob Cross 64
Hob on the Hill 64, *67*, 68
Hole of Horcum 45, *46–7*, 49, 72
Hutton-le-Hole 123

Ingleby Botton 99

Kettleness Point 38
Kilburn 18
Kilburn White Horse 16, 17–18,
    18

Levisham 6, 69, 123
Levisham Beck 45, 49
Levisham Moor 45, 69, 72
Low Mill 22, 25, 106, 111

Murk Esk 39, 44

Newtondale 69, 72
North Cheek, Robin Hood's Bay
    58, 63
North York Moors National Park
    8–10

North York Moors National Park
    Centre 88, 93

Osmotherley 50, 53

Port Mulgrave 34, *36*, 38

Roulston Scar *17*
Raisdale 94, 97
Ravenscar 83, 85, 100–102
Rievaulx Abbey 114, 121, *122*
Rievaulx Moor 117
Robin Hood's Bay 37, 58, 61, 63,
    83–7
Roseberry Topping *11*, 78, *81*, 82
Rosedale 26–8, 108
Rosedale Abbey *29*
Rosedale Abbey Bank 26
Round Hill, Botton Head 96, 99
Rudland Rigg 106, *108*
Runswick Bay 34, *35*, 37, 38
Rye, River 114, 121

Saltergate Bank 45, 49
Saltwick Nab 58, 61
Scarth Wood Moor *52*, 53
Seavy Pond 45
Siss Cross 88, 93
Skelton Tower *71*, 72
Staindale Water 6, 19, 20
Staithes 34, 37
Stoupe Brow Hill 87
Sutton Bank 16, 17

Urra Moor *14*

Wainstones 75, 96, 97, *98*, 99

Whisperdales 54, 57
Whitby 58, *59*, 61–63, 75
White Cross, Commondale 66, 68,
    88, 95